Table of Contents

CLASSICBEER **5** STYLESERIES

PORTER

TERRY FOSTER

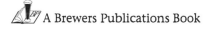 A Brewers Publications Book

Porter

Porter
By Terry Foster, Ph.D.
Classic Beer Style Series
Edited by Rob Henneke
Copyright 1992 by Terry Foster

ISBN 0-937381-28-4
Printed in the United States of America
10 9 8 7 6 5 4 3 2 1

Published by Brewers Publications,
a division of the Association of Brewers.
PO Box 1679, Boulder, Colorado 80306-1679 USA
Tel. (303) 447-0816 • FAX (303) 447-2825

Direct all inquiries/orders to the above address.

Cover design by Robert L. Schram
Cover photography by Michael Lichter, Michael Lichter Photography
Thanks to George Hanna, Oasis Brewery, Boulder, Colo., site of the
cover shoot.

Dedication

Porter has fascinated me for a long time. My wife has fascinated, intrigued and supported me for even a longer time. It is therefore fitting in this year of the 25th anniversary of our marriage that this book be dedicated to Lois Foster.

About the Author

Terry Foster was born in London and earned a Ph.D. in Organic Chemistry from London University. He has lived in the United States since 1977 and been brewing for over 30 years, through both the British *and* American homebrewing revolutions. Terry has written *Dr. Foster's Book of Beer* (England 1978), and *Pale Ale* (U.S.A. 1990, Brewers Publications), as well as many articles in both British and American brewing magazines. Currently he makes his living as a technical specialist for a manufacturer of mineral processing chemicals, a position which entails considerable international travel to countries raging from Australia to Zambia. He lives in Milford, Conn., with his wife and two children, in a 200-year-old house and likes reading, jazz, the Boston Red Sox, keeping fit, Maine lobsters, and free beer (not necessarily all together).

Introduction

I never wanted to write this book. I was afraid the research would take too long, and I would become so involved in it that I would not start writing. I worried that I would have too much material to put together in a logical and readable manner. And if I ever managed to do that and finished the book, I could never be satisfied with it. I am convinced that two days after publication I shall come across some long-hidden, but impeccably documented, facts which will dispute all the conclusions I have made. But here goes anyway!

I have been obsessed by porter ever since my first visit to a pub in London, the city where I was born. Like all the other pubs in those days, it had a little wooden sign over the door saying that the publican was, "Licensed to sell by retail porters, ales and stouts." But it was pale ale, and not porter, that I drank then. Although London was the home of porter, it was no longer brewed there, having died out during the 1930s.

In fact, in all the years I lived in England I *never* tasted a commercially-brewed porter. My first sampling was when I came to the United States in 1978. That was Narragansett

Porter, which by an eerie coincidence was brewed only a few miles from where my wife was born. By another coincidence, within less than a year of my leaving England, two breweries there decided to teach me a lesson and began brewing their own revivals of the style!

None of that surprised me, for porter has always been a contrary beer. It was not a style which just evolved, as most did, for it appears to have been deliberately designed to satisfy a particular market. As such it was the first clearly defined beer style, although we cannot say exactly what that style was. It was the first mass-produced beer, which permitted brewers to introduce some very important scientific and technological innovations. Those same innovations were at least partly responsible for the eventual demise of porter in England, as we shall see in the section on history.

Porter brewing was an integral part of the Industrial Revolution, in which Britain led the world, so it is not surprising that it also achieved popularity in other countries. Today versions of it are brewed in Eastern Europe, China, the Baltic region and North America. Porter was a foundation on which the English wholesale, or common, brewers were able to build substantial growth. Some of the original London porter brewers are still represented by name in Britain's largest brewing combines.

Through fueling the growth of the common brewers, porter played an important part in ensuring the decline of both the publican brewer and the craft of brewing at home. Yet it is a beer that fascinates homebrewers, quite a few of whom have spent hours trying to re-create it. Indeed, it has intrigued many beer enthusiasts, including the new breed of craftsman brewer who has started the micro and pubbreweries that have sprung up both here and in Britain in recent years. Several of these offer their own versions of porter, and it has even returned to its London home in a brewpub operated by a subsidiary of one of the major brewers.

Porter is not now produced in large volumes, having been displaced on one end by the pale beers it was invented to compete with and on the other end by the stouts that evolved from it. However, it still remains an important beer style, perhaps because of its importance in the history of brewing, and because it fills an important gap in the beer spectrum for the enthusiast. There are bottom-fermented versions of porter, but it is properly a top-fermented beer. It is therefore important as a representative of a once-dominant class of beers now almost entirely ousted by lager styles in most parts of the world outside of Great Britain and Ireland.

A further oddity about porter is that it and its great derivative stout came to be the most important Irish beer styles; porter died out in Ireland long after it ceased to be brewed in Britain. Moreover, it was clearly and unequivocally not just an English but a *London* brew, a draught beer drunk in London pubs.

Before porter became popular, London pubs probably were not much different from those in the country, little more than houses with a room or two set aside for drinking. They often were establishments that had been in place a long time, with their amenities slowly evolving to meet the drinker's needs. In the 18th and early 19th centuries, at the height of porter's popularity, the population of London grew rapidly, creating a demand for many more pubs.

Some brewers responded to this demand by building much larger pubs. These were often custom designed by architects, a step that represented a very radical change in the evolution of the English pub. This new approach became a trend that is still followed by modern brewers, although it reached its zenith in the latter part of the 18th century in the magnificent carved wood and cut glass extravaganzas of the so-called gin palaces. By that time porter no longer dominated the London scene, but there is little doubt that the capital generated from its sales was largely responsible for this development.

There is another reason why I did not want to write about porter. It made me nostalgic for my youth and the pubs where I learned to drink beer! However, there is one very good reason why this book has been written: Porter must not be allowed to die. It is a unique beer with a color, subtlety and complexity of flavor all its own. Porter encapsulates the magical variety of beer which is so often ignored by modern commercial manufacturers. Whether you are a micro or a homebrewer, a version of this style should be in your brewing book!

1

A History Of Porter

ORIGINS

Simplicity is a virtue in many things. But a simple beer is only a thirst-quencher. A great beer is that too, but much more, for it should be a densely-woven tapestry of flavors, surprising and pleasing at every turn and never wholly predictable. Porter certainly fits that criterion as a beer; as a part of history it is also intriguing, multifaceted and enigmatic.

One of the oddest things about porter is how clearly and precisely the reason for its invention and the date and place of its origin have been defined by so many historians. There were three types of beer available in the early 18th century, and the drinker liked a mixture of them. This mixture was known as "three threads," and the publican had to draw it to order from three separate casks. This was obviously a very laborious procedure, so in 1722, a gentleman by the name of Ralph Harwood, proprietor of the Bell Brewhouse in Shoreditch, East London, came up with the idea of a beer which had all the characteristics of three threads, yet could be served from a single cask. It was called

"Mr. Harwood's Entire" or "Entire Butt" and was first sold at a pub called the Blue Last on Great Eastern Street in Shoreditch.

The new beer permitted the publican to offer a much faster service to his customers, many of whom were manual workers. Since there were few machines in those days, the physical demands on workers were high, and they needed constant refreshment with little time to spare. The new speedily-served beer exactly suited these requirements, and the custom of the Blue Last expanded very quickly. In order to express his satisfaction with his increased business, the publican called it porter, since porters were his best customers for the new beer.

This whole story seems to be just a little too neat and precise in its details. The derivation of the names is probably correct, and it is surely true that the manual workers had a great thirst for beer. Benjamin Franklin worked at a London printer in the 1720s and recorded that the printers drank six pints of strong beer during every working day, including one before breakfast! However, I have difficulty in believing the rest of the story, for there seem to be too many holes in the other facts.

As far as I can see, every writer who has told this story got the idea that it was Harwood who invented porter from the same source: John Bickerdyke's *Curiosities of Ale and Beer*, published 150 years after the arrival of porter. Moreover, these writers are unable to agree as to which beers were the constituents of three threads. At least six are quoted: ale, beer, twopenny, brown ale, stale brown ale, and pale ale. In fact, one publication of the 1720s stated there were at least 23 different types of beer sold in London, while another reports that an alehouse of the time sported a sign saying, "Here is to be sold two threads, three threads, four threads, and six threads"!

Further, porter was being sold all over London within a very short time after 1722. Many brewers were producing it and prospering in the process. The inventive Mr. Harwood, whom we might have expected to be the most successful of them all, seems to have disappeared from the scene as he is not mentioned in later listings of porter brewers. It is also hardly credible that he would have been willing to pass on the secret of brewing Entire to his competitors, or that they could have stolen it from him so easily.

What then is the truth of the origin of porter? We shall probably never be certain because we are talking about events of almost three hundred years ago. The brewing process, though widely practiced, was not at all well understood. Not even simple instruments like the thermometer and hydrometer were used, and brewers had no idea of the effectiveness of their mashing techniques, nor of the role of yeast in fermentation. It is therefore not easy to determine precise details of the nature of beer and brewing processes of those times. This problem is complicated by the fact that even words had different meanings then. For example, stale was often used to describe beer, but meant mature or mellow, rather than the modern rancid connotation of the word.

Despite these difficulties, some beer historians offer another, more plausible account of the origin of porter. What follows is my version of that account. At the beginning of the 18th century, the technique of sparging was unknown. The malt was mashed several times, with each lot of wort drawn off separately, and boiled and fermented to give different beers. These were usually known as strong, common and small. Since there was no way to measure beer strength in those days, the quality of such beers, even when made from the same amount of malt, could obviously vary widely.

By 1700, ale (in the original sense of beer brewed without hops) had disappeared entirely, and all beer was brewed with at least some hops. However, it appears that in many cases the hop rate was fairly minimal (one-half pound/ barrel, or a little less than one ounce/five U.S. gallons) so that the beers would not have been very bitter. This began to change in the early part of the century as transport started to improve, and many beers from other parts of the country became available in London. Most important of all, a good deal of this beer was Burton pale ale, a heavier-hopped beer than the pale ales brewed in London. The strong March and October ales used up to two pounds/barrel, about four ounces/five U.S. gallons.

While the imported beers would have been more expensive than the local brews, and were often mixed with cheaper London beers, there seems little doubt that drinkers did develop a taste for more highly-hopped beers. The London brown beer brewers had to respond to this demand, but they did not want to simply become pale ale brewers themselves. They wanted to brew a dark beer using cheap brown malt and plenty of hops, so that they could satisfy the drinker's demands and keep down the cost. They may also have been aware that London water, high in bicarbonates, was ideally suited to brewing with dark malts but was not at all desirable for pale malt.

There is another aspect of this story, for it appears that around this time the London brewers had reached "critical mass." At the beginning of the 18th century, the British brewing industry was already dominated by wholesale, or common brewers, with less than 1 percent of total commercial output being produced by publican brewers. London was by far the biggest single section of the market, consuming about 20 percent of total British output; the city had 194 common brewers with an *average* annual production of 8,500 barrels of strong and small beer. In other words, they were already at the size of a fairly big modern microbrewery and needed only the right product to make the jump up to the next order of magnitude, which was mass as opposed to craftsman production.

Porter was exactly the brew which enabled them to make that jump. It required only cheap ingredients, could only be produced on a large scale since it needed long storage, and became immensely popular, ensuring a good return on the invested capital. As we shall see under the section on the growth of the brewers, only the bigger brewers could take advantage of porter's popularity because of the large capital investments required.

It also seems likely that porter brewing represented a technical advance in that the runnings from each mash were no longer treated separately but were combined to give a single beer. If so, that is where the name Entire originated, indicating that the beer was brewed from an Entire gyle, that is, from a mixture of all the worts. The evidence for this is inferential; porter was certainly being produced in this manner later in the century. The technique would have meant that the brewer could produce much more strong beer from the same quantity of malt than if he were operating the old "parti-gyle" system. Remember that actual original gravities could not be determined at that time, so that there was no clear definition of what constituted strength.

There is another important point to be considered here. Beer prices were actually controlled by statute and not by market forces. Therefore, an Entire-gyle system of brewing would effectively permit the brewer to charge strong beer prices for what would have been small beer under the old system of brewing. Clearly, the coupling of this with the tremendous popularity of porter put the porter brewer at enormous financial advantage compared to his competition.

A few last words on the names Porter and Entire. Although porter was both imported into this country and later brewed here, the name Entire was not often used in America. In England breweries were still making wide use of Entire in their pub advertising by the end of the 19th century, often on a huge board running right across the top of the pub. Others used only the word Porter, but some advertised both Entire and Porter on the facade of the same pub! This does not mean that they were talking about different beers, but it does mean that there was still some confusion in the drinker's mind. This is not surprising, for both terms had been in wide use since the inception of porter brewing. In those days there would have been no point-of-sale advertising for draught beers, so the brewers may simply have used their external advertising to assure the customer that they served the beer he wanted, whatever he called it.

THE NATURE OF PORTER

This is the nitty-gritty of porter, the Holy Grail for the brewing enthusiast who wants to re-create the beer in all its original glory. What was it really like? Logic tells us that we shall never know, because we will never know exactly how it was brewed, nor will we ever have the same raw materials. More importantly, since we can't taste the beer produced in 1722, we shall never be able to tell whether we have matched it, *even if we have!* Yet it is a question which I, for one, cannot let go, so I am going to spend some time on it here.

We have already discussed the basics of what porter was: a beer brewed only from brown malt, long-stored and heavily hopped. That definition raises a lot more questions than it answers, the first of which is, "What was brown malt?" The information we can derive from the literature is pretty sketchy. A publication called *The London and Country Brewer*, first published in 1735, is the best source. Indeed, as one writer has remarked, this was probably the first really technical publication on brewing.

The anonymous writer tells us that it was a high-dried malt, with the drying often being overdone so "that the farinaceous part loses a great deal of its essential salts." It seems he had some idea of what kind of extract a malt should yield, and the inference is that brown malt gave less extract than lower-dried malts, such as pale. It would be nearly 50 years later before this was proven scientifically.

Since porter was produced only from brown malt, it is clear that the diastatic activity of the malt could not have been completely destroyed. It was surely not as dark as modern high-dried or roasted malts. In fact, the term brown malt was widely used in England in the 18th century, but this referred to a product with no residual diastatic activity, which was intermediate in color between black and crystal malts, suggesting that it was pretty close in character to modern chocolate malt.

The point I am making is that porter was not a *black* beer as some people seem to think. Indeed, when brown malt ceased to be used, and black beers were available, brewers had a great deal of difficulty in brewing porter with what was perceived to be its proper color. A good many of them solved this problem by adulterating the beer with all kinds of noxious colorants. This would seem to suggest, as does *The London and Country Brewer*, that porter was at least translucent, probably with a ruby-red rather than a black-brown hue.

What about the strength of porter? This is an impossible question to answer, since there are no numbers available for the original versions of porter. The relatively primitive brewing techniques of the time probably meant that there was considerable variation in both original and finishing gravities, both between and within breweries.

The only direct evidence on strength comes almost 50

years later when two writers, John Richardson (1777, 1784) and James Baverstock (1785), published accounts of the application of the hydrometer in the brewing process. Richardson quoted numbers on various kinds of beers; porter had OG 1.071 (17.2 °Plato) and FG 1.018 (4.5 °Plato), while strong ale had OG 1.110 (26.8 °Plato), FG 1.052 (12.8 °Plato). Though the OG for porter is pretty high by modern standards, it was significantly lower than strong ale. It would have contained almost as much alcohol because it was considerably more attentuated than the strong ale.

Unfortunately, we do not know how representative Richardson's results were, so the porter he quotes may or may not have been typical of those available. Later figures from the early to mid-19th century give a range of OG values for common London porter (1.050 to 1.067; 12.3 to 16.3 °Plato). However, by that time brewing techniques had changed substantially, largely as a result of Richardson's own work, which had shown that brown malt was a poor value for the money in terms of its yield of extract. Still, it does seem likely that the original had OG somewhere in the range 1.050 to 1.070 (12.3 to 17 °Plato), with most brews probably falling in the range 1.060 to 1.070 (14.7 to 17 °Plato).

Actual mashing techniques must have been pretty primitive for brewers were not yet using the thermometer, although Fahrenheit had invented his mercury-in-glass instrument in 1714. However, as the porter brewers grew, they gradually adopted technological advances. By 1762, Michael Combrune was quoting porter mashing temperatures of 130 to 150 degrees F (54.4 to 65.5 degrees C) for the first mash and 165 to 183 degrees F (74 to 84 degrees C) for the last mash.

A more detailed mashing procedure is given by another writer for the time, "When the grist for porter became a standard of equal parts of brown, amber and pale malts," which was presumably around 1800. First mash was at 150 degrees F (65.5 degrees C) with two barrels of water per quarter (72 Imperial gallons/330 pounds malt) for one hour. Wort was run off, and three hours later the second mash was conducted at 160 degrees F (71 degrees C) for one-half hour, with one barrel of water per quarter (36 Imperial gallons/ 330 pounds). The third mash water (1 1/4 barrels/quarter, or 45 Imperial gallons/330 pounds) was run in 2 1/2 hours later at 180 degrees F (82 degrees C) for 1 1/2 hours. The three worts took three to four hours boiling, giving 3 1/2 barrels of wort with OG 1.067 (16.3 °Plato), which was fermented down to 1.019 (4.8 °Plato).

The next point to consider is how porter was hopped. Again, we are going to have to make some guesses because we know that the early porter brewers had no understanding of the chemistry of hops. There is no evidence that late hopping was practiced, so it is probable that the hops were added at the beginning of the boil and extraction of the bittering principles was fairly good. Indeed, it is suggested by one writer that the hops could be boiled up to four times! That would presumably only have happened if each running from the mash was boiled separately, immediately on collection, before being finally mixed together to form an Entire gyle.

The actual nature of the hops and their alpha acid content is unknown. None of the varieties now in use were available in the first half of the 18th century, and a good many that came after that time, such as Jones, Williams, Farnham and Canterbury White Bines, Cooper's White and Amos Early Bird, are now no longer grown. The only pre-20th century hop varieties still in existence are the Fuggle and the Goldings, and even the Fuggle was not discovered until 1875, by which time porter was already well on its way out of popularity.

The Goldings hop, first cultivated in the 1780s, is really the only variety we know that could have been extensively used to brew porter. Since it is actually regarded as the classic pale ale variety, there is a good chance that it was *not* used in darker beers. What we can perhaps assume is that the hops that were used for porter were fairly similar to Goldings in terms of their alpha acid content, around 4 to 5 percent alpha acid.

We do have some idea as to much hops were used. *The London and Country Brewer* quotes three pounds per hogshead (54 Imperial gallons). That is about 1 1/2 pounds/U.S. barrel or almost four ounces/five U.S. gallons. If we take the conservative figures of 4 percent alpha acid and 25 percent utilization, this translates to 60 IBU, a level matched by few modern beers. For comparison, Guinness Extra Stout runs at about 50 IBU, and in *Pale Ale* I recommended that IPA, a beer whose flavors *should* be dominated by hop bitterness, run no more than 55 IBU! In short, even allowing for the relatively high original gravity of porter, this would have been a very bitter beer indeed. Confirmation of this level of hopping comes from other sources; the 3 1/2 barrels of porter obtained in the detailed mashing procedure above used six to seven pounds of hops, which also works out to about four ounces/five U.S. gallons.

The final areas to consider are fermentation and storage. The first is easily disposed of, for there is very little in the literature on it. That is not surprising because it would be 150 years after porter's invention before Pasteur finally uncovered the role of yeast in fermentation. All we can say is that top-fermenting yeasts were used, and that the brewer's only method of temperature control was to avoid brewing entirely in the hot summer months!

The question of storage is another matter, for long storage of porter was undoubtedly an important feature of its production. The beer was kept for several months, perhaps as much as a year for the better kinds. At first, it was stored in wooden casks, but not long after porter's first appearance the technology for building large wooden vats became available, and porter could be stored in vast quantities. The use of such vats, with a high volume to surface area ratio, permitted good temperature control of the stored beer.

However, there is a good deal of evidence that such storage in wood would have resulted in a so-called "subacid" flavor. The porous wood tended to retain various species of microflora, such as *Brettanomyces* and lactobacilli, that would have produced small amounts of acid in the beer. This is somewhat similar to what happens with Belgian lambic beers, though the effect with porter was probably much less marked.

So, to summarize our picture of original porter we have:

- Made from only a high-dried, but not roasted, brown malt
- Original gravity probably 1.060 to 1.070 (14.7 to 17 °Plato)
- A three-stage mash with the first at around 150 degrees F (65.5 degrees C); all runnings collected together
- High hop rate of around four ounces/five gallons added at start of boil
- Fermentation at ambient temperatures with a top yeast; high attenuation with FG around one-quarter of OG
- Stored for several months in wooden vats
- Translucent, deep red-brown in color, high in alcohol (six to seven percent by volume), fairly low in residual sugar, high in hop bitterness with background acid notes

That is as far as we can go with the original. If you want

to try and match it yourself, the above information should give you a good jumping-off point. There is, however, another source you might want to look at before beginning, and that's the booklet put out by an English group of home-brewers, Durden Park Beer Circle, on how to make *Old British Beers*. They list three recipes for porter, including an "Original" (1750), an "1800," and a "Whitbread's 1850."

Their Original is notably different from any of my versions. It has OG 1.090 (21.5 °Plato) and uses no less than eight ounces Goldings hops per five U.S. gallons. Assuming these contain five percent alpha acid, and utilization is only 25 percent, this calculates out to around 150 IBU, an *extremely* high level of bitterness by today's standards.

Both their 1800 and 1850 versions are more similar to mine with OG 1.060 (14.7 °Plato), and hop rates at close to four ounces/five U.S. gallons. The latter is particularly interesting, for it is based on information obtained from Whitbread themselves. Whitbread was one of the great London porter brewers and led the field in porter production for a good many years, so this recipe is about as authentic as we can ever hope to get.

As I said in the Introduction, I am certain that somewhere out there is some definitive piece of evidence as to the true nature of porter in its original form, and that it will come to light immediately after this book is published. If you are the one to find this brewer's version of the Philosopher's Stone, please pass it on to me *immediately!*

There is one final comment I must make on this subject. Writing in 1824, a certain Bennington Mowbray bemoaned the decline of private brewing in England. In particular, he complained that the Londoner's liking for porter was a huge barrier to private brewing in the city, "for London porter, which no private family, so far as I have heard, has succeeded in brewing to perfection." The idea that porter could not be satisfactorily brewed in the home may be taken as a warning; I prefer to put it to you as a challenge!

GROWTH OF PORTER AND ITS BREWERS

The history of porter and the men who made it is fascinating, for it deals with the part that beer has played in the development of Western culture. Conversely, of course, much of porter's growth was the result of profound changes in the nature of British society. It is also a microcosm of how our industries have developed; events in porter's history explain the structure of the modern brewing industry, not only in Britain, but in the other major Western countries.

Porter is intimately tied in with the Industrial Revolution, in which Britain led the world. Through the growth it enabled the brewers to achieve, it was instrumental in the development and technological application of a number of important scientific advances. Despite my origins, I am not being chauvinistic about the importance of porter's part in brewing history. In the 18th century the British brewing industry was far ahead of that even in the other famous brewing nations, such as Germany and the United States, neither of which caught up with Britain's technology until the mid-19th century.

To illustrate this last point, Gabriel Sedlmayer, the great Munich brewer who played such an important part in the development of bottom-fermented lagers, visited England in the 1830s. A writer of the time called this visit a milestone in the history of the German brewing industry, and innovations such as the use of the steam engine, saccharometer and thermometer were rapidly taken up in Germany and Austria. At that time British brewers had been using all these for 50 years or more!

The most significant thing about porter was the scale of operations of its brewers. During the 100 years or so after 1722, the number of common brewers in London actually decreased. We have already seen that there were 194 in the city around 1700, by 1750 there were 165, and by 1800 their numbers had fallen to 127, decreasing again to 115 in 1830. This trend has continued until today when, apart from a few brewpubs, only four brewing companies remain in the London area: Fuller, Grand Metropolitan (Watney), Guinness and Young. Guinness, of course, has its own intriguing part in the history of porter, but is a relative newcomer to London, while there is some doubt as to whether Watney will continue its brewing operations for much longer.

The total production of beer in the United Kingdom actually fell during this period, going from 15 million barrels in 1722 down to 13 million in 1786. This is a little surprising for it was a time when the populations of the cities were growing, and people were moving from the land to the cities to work in the proliferating factories as the Industrial Revolution gathered steam. In fact, many of the urban poor were drinking gin rather than beer. Gin was so cheap that one innkeeper advertised that you get could get "dead drunk for twopence" at a time when just one quart of porter cost threepence!

Excessive gin drinking had disastrous social effects which are not really a part of the porter story, but the popularity of the spirit undoubtedly influenced the development of the brewing industry. For example, it is recorded that in 1722 per capita consumption in England was one-half gallon of spirits and one barrel of beer. A little over 100 years later in 1833 the corresponding figures were nine-tenths gallon of spirits and one-half barrel of beer! Since most of this gin seems to have been consumed in the larger cities, especially London, those figures are probably considerably lower than the actual per capita consumption in London.

Nevertheless, production of beer by the London brewers had increased from about 1 1/2 million barrels in 1700 to around two million barrels by 1786. Since the number of brewers had decreased, it is clear that there had been a significant surge in the size of individual brewers. In England and Wales as a whole, publican and private brewers still operated on an impressive scale, for as late as 1830 it was estimated that private brewers produced anywhere from 20 to 50 percent of the total beer brewed. However, in London the situation was very different; in the cramped conditions of the city private brewing was impractical, and the publican brewer could not compete with the porter manufacturers. In 1830, the 115 London common brewers brewed 95 percent of the beer produced in the capital.

Even the number of 115 is misleading, for many of those were still quite small concerns. Around the beginning of the 19th century, a remarkable concentration had taken place in porter brewing with the bulk of it being produced by less than a dozen large companies, notably Barclay Perkins, Felix Calvert, Combe Delafield, Meux Reid, Truman Hanbury & Buxton, and Whitbread. Some of these were long-established breweries. Truman, for example, having commenced brewing as far back as 1683. Others started after the invention of porter. Whitbread began in 1742 as a brewer of pale and amber ales, building his famous Chiswell Street porter brewery just a few years later.

In fact, Truman's company had been rescued in 1789 by a group of Quakers, and another of these names arose through an established brewery being bought up by what were essentially financial interests. Ralph Thrale was one of the original porter brewers, and his Southwark brewery went back as far as 1616. On his son's death in 1781, the brewery was taken over by a group of Quakers led by Robert Barclay (from America!) and included David Barclay (a banker), as well as John Perkins who had been the technical manager of the brewery. The sale of the Thrale brewery was the source of the famous remark of the lexicographer Dr. Johnson who said to a prospective bidder, "Sir, we are not here to sell a parcel of boilers and vats, but the potentiality of growing rich beyond the dreams of avarice."

This story gives us a feel of both the cost and the rewards of being a successful porter brewer. According to *The London Tradesman*, it was estimated that it took more capital to start up as a porter brewer than it did to get into any other trade except for banking. The clearest illustration of that is the size of the storage vats built by the porter brewers.

The porter breweries grew so rapidly because they were able to move up to a much higher level of production than had been seen previously in the brewing industry. This jump took them to the point where their operations were large enough to permit them to achieve economies of scale and to dominate the market, thus generating sufficient cash flow to fund further expansion. The ability to store beer in vast quantities was one of the critical factors in this expansion.

It was difficult to do so in 1720, for it was not possible to manufacture large vessels, apart from coopered wooden casks. Even the biggest of these could not hold much over a hundred gallons. But the techniques of coopering large wooden vats, as opposed to casks, was quickly developed. By 1736, one London brewer, Parsons, had installed vats capable of holding 1500 barrels (over 60,000 U.S. gallons). Thrale was quick to follow with similar-sized vessels, and Whitbread was building vessels holding 4,000 barrels each less than 10 years later.

The ownership of bigger vats soon became the porter

brewer's status symbol and offered him an opportunity for promotional events. Henry Thrale built one so large that 100 people were able to dine in it at its inauguration. Not to be outdone, Meux erected one large enough to take 200 diners in 1790! The ultimate in such vats was put together by the same brewer in 1795; it had a capacity of 20,000 barrels (about 860,000 U.S. gallons!).

Meux' eagerness to lead the field in this aspect of brewing technology led to a disaster at the Tottenham Court Road Brewery. In October of 1814, one of the coopered porter vats burst, and its spilled contents did considerable damage, knocking down brewery walls and demolishing adjacent buildings, as well as killing eight people. The causes of their deaths were variously reported as "drowning, injury, poisoning by porter fumes or drunkenness."

Whitbread was more innovative; he introduced an interesting variation on the storage vat. This was the cistern, which was simply an underground tank. Lining the cisterns was a problem that was eventually solved by using specially glazed tiles obtained from Wedgwood and fixing them in place with a cement specifically designed to stand up to long contact with porter. Several of these formed part of the famous Great Tun Room, completed in 1760 and built to such a standard that it survived the heavy bombing of London at the start of the Second World War.

Other technical advances were taken up by Whitbread's brewery as it expanded. One writer, in 1819 to 1820, describes the brewery in some detail and describes how both the cisterns and the fermentation vessels were fitted with copper coils, through which cold water could be circulated, so that the temperatures of their contents could be controlled. However, heat exchangers had not been invented, and after boiling the wort was still cooled by standing in long shallow vessels or "coolships."

Interior of a coolship, or large wort cooling vessel. Photo courtesy of Adolf Coors Co.

Whitbread soon became the foremost London brewer and before the end of the 18th century became the first to reach an annual output of 200,000 barrels (nearly nine million U.S. gallons)! He didn't remain the biggest brewer for very long. In 1812, his production had fallen back to 122,000 barrels while Truman had turned out 150,000 barrels, Meux 180,000 barrels, and Barclay Perkins led the field with a huge 270,000 barrels (about 12 million U.S. gallons)! In contrast, the largest London ale brewer only managed a mere 20,000 barrels in 1813.

Growth continued with Barclay breaking the 300,000 barrel mark in 1820. By 1827, it was finally leveling off; Barclay had declined to 276,000 barrels per year, Truman had increased to 211,000, Whitbread had pulled back up to 163,000, and Meux's output had fallen to 165,000 barrels.

In fact, this was about the summit of porter brewing in London; its decline was about to begin. Although porter itself went into decline, many of its brewers had become so well established that they were able to survive by adapting to the competitive pressures, as we shall see later.

One very interesting thing about this growth of the brewers was that it was achieved despite a remarkable stability in the price of the product. In 1722, it cost threepence per quart, rising to three-and-a-halfpence in 1761 in response to duty increases, then to fourpence per quart in 1780, a price which was still holding in 1799. The increase in 1761 was notable in that it was the first made by brewers and publicans without the sanction of the authorities. It was perhaps the first instance of beer prices being determined by market forces alone. Nevertheless, one writer has calculated that over this period of almost 80 years, the gross profit on a barrel of porter remained constant at 13 shillings!

The only way to increase profits in the face of a constant price was to increase output. One way to do this, as we have seen, was to utilize advances in brewing technology. Another was for the brewery to lock in its own retail outlets. This "tying" of pubs, as it is called, could be done by either direct ownership of the leases of premises, or through lending money to the purchaser with the condition that he sold only beer brewed by the lender. The tied trade began to become important in London during the 18th century. It is recorded that by 1820 Thrale (Barclay), Whitbread and Truman each held ties in more than half of the total outlets they supplied. Indeed, a Parliamentary Select Committee reported in 1817 that nearly half the licenses in London were tied.

The significance of this is that the cornerstone of the modern British brewing industry is the tied house. As competition intensified in the 19th century, brewers moved more and more into the ownership of pubs. One result of this was that in the 20th century the only way for a brewer to grow was to buy up another brewery, close its brewing operations, and fill its pubs with its own brand of beer.

An interesting example of this involves both the Barclay Perkins brewery I have already talked about and John Courage, who started brewing in London a little after Barclay and Perkins took over Henry Thrale's brewery, plus three other 18th century brewers from other parts of the country. The diagram represents brewery takeovers. For convenience only breweries actually still in existence in the 20th century are included:

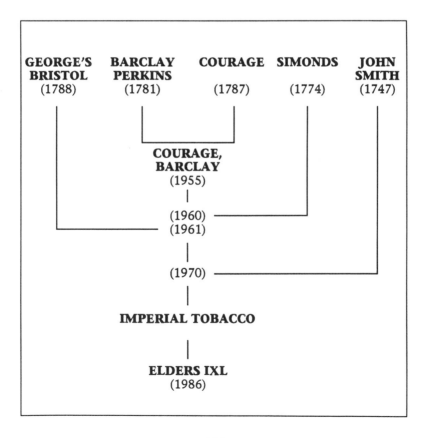

More takeovers occurred than are actually shown; several breweries were themselves the products of a series of buy outs and mergers. In all, it required over 50 takeovers during *this century alone* to create the Courage brewing arm of Elders!

There are a few other interesting points about these breweries. George started as a porter brewery in the great port of Bristol and depended on export trade for much of its growth, though neither Simonds nor Smith were porter brewers. Oddly enough, John is the same family as Samuel Smith, which is still an independent company, and was one of those taking part in the revival of porter brewing in England in the 1970s. Even odder is the fact that both brewers are based in Tadcaster, Yorkshire, where the hard water is best suited to pale beer brewing!

Barclay Perkins we have seen already, but they are also notable as being the originators of Imperial Russian Stout. This vintage-dated beer, one of the strongest brewed in England today, probably developed from porter, as did stouts in general. I have already described the antiquity of the Barclay brewery, but Courage perhaps goes back even further. Although Courage bought the brewery in the Horselydown area of Southwark in 1787, brewing may have been carried out on the site since Elizabethan times. It was then owned by a man who is said to have been the inspiration for Shakespeare's character Sir John Falstaff.

Both the Barclay and Courage breweries were on the southern side of the River Thames in Southwark, which is the area where many of the original beer brewers settled, when the technique of brewing with hops first came to England. For centuries Southwark was the center of England's hop trade. The Horselydown brewery must have been pretty small when John Courage bought it, for it only cost him a little over 600 pounds, whereas Barclay's company must

25

The Horselydown Brewery of Southwark, England, has a long history of brewing. Photo by Terry Foster.

have been worth close to a thousand times this figure at that time!

The Anchor Brewhouse, as Courage renamed it, still exists, though it was rebuilt twice in the 19th century. Brewing ceased there in 1981, and it now only houses offices, but as the photographs show, it is still an impressive building fronting onto the river right by Tower Bridge.

Elders, of course, is actually an Australian company, and it is odd that an empire built on porter brewing should now be in such hands, since porter does not seem to have ever been a particularly important Australian brew. They are also involved in a deal, not yet finalized, with Grand Metropolitan, the company which absorbed both Truman and Watney. Under this deal, sparked by new laws restricting the number of tied houses any one brewery can hold, Grand Met would sell its breweries to Elders in exchange for an interest in a pub-owning chain. Both this chain and Grand Metropolitan's other pubs would be contracted to take their beer from Elders for five years, making Elders the second biggest brewing group after Bass.

The final curiosity is that the company recently changed its name to Fosters Brewing. I have no connection with it! There *was* a Foster brewing in London in the 18th century, but it was a small operation, and I have not been able to find out whether it brewed porter or ale, though I am pretty sure it was not one of my relations.

PORTER BREWING OUTSIDE OF LONDON

The London brewers were quick to build on their success and to ship porter to other parts of Britain. Regional brewers reacted to this new competition by producing their own versions, although not as swiftly as might have been expected. This may be because there was not such an overwhelming demand for porter in other cities, but it could simply have been that they had difficulty in matching the quality of London porter. Water quality could well have been a significant factor, for many of the larger regional brewing centers were situated in areas where the water was high in gypsum, or permanent hardness. This was not as well suited to porter manufacture as was London water whose predominant characteristic was temporary hardness due to the presence of bicarbonates leached from the chalky soils of the Southeast. Sheffield, in Yorkshire, was the first provincial city in which porter was brewed. One writer says this was in 1744, but a more definitive reference states that it was 1758, the brewer being Thomas Rawson. The brewery stayed in existence until it was destroyed in a 1940 German air raid, although the company itself was taken over. The buyer was subsequently swallowed by Joshua Tetley, which is now an arm of the giant Allied Breweries.

The Scottish city of Glasgow seems to have been next on the list. Appropriately, Glasgow's water was much softer

than that of Edinburgh, Scotland's capital. Porter brewing apparently started there in 1760, but the product does not appear to have been up to London standards, for in 1775 Murdoch, Warroch and Company imported a London-trained brewer. Inside a year this company was turning out a top quality porter. Then, they promptly fired their teacher, though with true Scottish generosity they did give him a ticket back to London! He paid them back by going to work for a competitor, John Struthers, until stopped from doing so by a court interdict obtained by his original employer on the grounds that his contract had contained a clause excluding him from passing on his knowledge to any other Glasgow brewer! But it was too late. By the time of the court order, he had managed to teach Struthers his art, and this brewery too was producing a porter as good as any London brew.

Outside of London, Bristol was probably the most important English porter-brewing center, but it is not clear when it was first produced in that city. The most famous Bristol porter brewery was that of Philip George, which I mentioned in the last section as starting in 1788. However, George apparently bought an existing porter brewery, so the beer was certainly being made there before that date. By 1773, there were already three porter brewers in Dublin, and London porter had been exported to Ireland from about 1750. Most of that trade would have gone through Bristol, so it seems likely that some enterprising Bristol brewer would have made his own version of the beer before the 1770s.

The Irish brewers had an important part to play in the porter story. By 1770, English imports into Ireland were growing, and the local brewers were struggling to compete. In part this was because the English exporters received a drawback, or refund, on the English duty and paid only a very small Irish import duty. Beer brewed in Ireland, on the other hand, paid duty at a much higher rate. In fact, Arthur Guinness, who founded his Dublin brewery in 1759, is supposed to have told the Irish House of Commons that he would move his brewery to Wales if they did not soon change this unfair arrangement!

It may well be that the Irish industry was simply not as efficient as that in London, coupled with the fact that the Irish drinker seemed to be as fond of porter as the Londoner, and most of the Irish brewers were still producing ale. Indeed, around this time they began to brew more and more porter and to take a larger share of their own market. There is evidence that they rapidly caught up with the English brewers in their technology, and English imports peaked in the 1790s.

Guinness was brewing only porter by 1803, and by 1838 they led a substantial Irish export trade *to* England. This company's slice of the English market was to grow enormously in the future, particularly with the increase in the market for stout, originally a strong version of porter. During the 19th century Guinness' Dublin brewery became the largest in the world. It was the first brewing concern to become a registered public company in Britain and built a second brewery on the outskirts of London in 1936. Today its famous Extra Stout is Britain's most widely-consumed dark beer.

Another very important part of the porter story was, and is, America. Stanley Baron, in his definitive history *Brewed in America*, says that on the whole "Porter never gained popular success in America, either because it was more expensive to start with than the local ale, or because drinking tastes had diverged from those in England." It is true that porter never dominated any segment of the American market as it did London, yet it was widely brewed in this country. And American porter brewing has a continuity that its English counterpart does not, for Yuengling's version of the beer has been brewed since the 19th century, interrupted only briefly by Prohibition.

It is not clear exactly when commercial brewing started in America, although it was surely under way by 1630. Before 1635 a Captain Robert Sedgwick was licensed as a common brewer in the Massachusetts Bay Colony. His name is notable, since his brother was a brewer in Southwark where, as we have seen, both Courage and Barclay Perkins brewed porter.

Brewing spread quite widely in the colonies, although a good deal of their beer was imported from England. In 1702, a visitor to Williamsburg, Virginia, reported being served some English stout. In the 1730s, a Philadelphia brewery was also offering a stout, which fetched a premium over strong ale. This may be misleading in that the term stout was not much used in England at that time and may have simply meant a very strong beer, rather than the black derivative of porter we call stout today.

George Washington was almost as much a father of the American porter brewing industry as he was of the country. As early as 1760, he is recorded as both buying imported porter locally and ordering it directly from England. However, as emotions heated up before the Revolution, he was a party to a 1769 agreement to ban the import of British goods including porter and other beers. In contrast, the British Army found it impossible to continue the Revolutionary War without ordering considerable supplies of porter. Both Felix Calvert and Henry Thrale were contracted to provide 5,000 butts, or about 600,000 U.S. gallons, to keep the mercenary troops going.

It is possible porter was brewed in the United States before the Revolution, but it was certainly being made there after that. According to Baron, the first U.S. porter brewer was Robert Hare, the son of a brewer in Limehouse, East London, and therefore a true "Limey"! Hare started in Philadelphia in 1776, and Washington was reported to have been particularly fond of his brew. In 1781, porter was also being produced in Massachusetts, since the Speaker of the Massachusetts House of Representatives made a present of it to Washington. It is worth noting that in this period most American brewers were using a sizeable proportion of molasses in their grists.

Pennsylvania seems to have been the hotbed for American porter, for both Philadelphia and Pittsburgh brewed more of this beer than ale. Indeed, Jefferson bought porter while he was living in Philadelphia, though this was probably for his guests, since he apparently preferred wine to beer. However, he did brew beer at Monticello in 1813; he owned copies of both *The London and Country Brewer* and Michael Combrune's *Theory and Practice of Brewing*. Given that Jefferson's books formed the nucleus of the Library of Congress, this is a fitting tribute to the importance of brewing in American culture.

Porter may not have dominated the United States market, but almost every brewer who started in the United States after the Revolution produced porter as well as ale. In 1812, Matthew Vassar was offering his own Poughkeepsie porter, along with the Philadelphia variety and London Brown Stout. Porter was also on sale in St. Louis in 1813 and was being brewed in Cincinnati (1816), Chicago (1833), and Cleveland (1850), while Meldrum and Co., a Boston brewer, was offering a pale porter in 1832.

Even in the West the story was the same. In 1849, at least one San Francisco brewer was producing porter, as did the first Seattle brewery, which was founded some time before 1864. The first Phoenix brewery, founded in 1878,

Matthew Vassar, son of James Vassar who came to Poughkeepsie in 1793 to set up a brewhouse. Matthew Vassar expanded the family brewery after his father's death and was soon producing 20,000 barrels of ale, beer and Porter—quite an increase from his father's 15 gallons of ale daily. From *One Hundred Years of Brewing (H.S. Rich & Co. Publishers 1903).*

brewed ale and porter as well as beer. One of the most famous of lager brewers, Adolph Coors, figures in our story. Before he actually opened a brewery he ran a bottling business and advertised "Bottled Porter" for sale!

Of course, lager beer was eventually to displace porter and ale in America. The first brewing of this variety of beer took place in Philadelphia in 1840. At first its popularity was limited to communities of German immigrants, and it only began to displace English-style ales and porter after the 1850s. In fact, lager beer arrived in America at a crucial point in the development of the country's brewing industry.

33

Coors Porter, bottled by Adolf
Coors in a pre-brewing venture.
Photo and label courtesy of
Adolf Coors Co.

In 1850, there were 431 breweries in the United States, churning out a total of 750,000 barrels per year. That was an average of less than 2,000 barrels per year each; compare that with the 8,500 barrels per year average for London common brewers 150 years earlier, and it is clear that the U.S. industry was relatively backward. Further, the industry was highly concentrated, for Philadelphia and New York accounted for no less than 85 percent of total American output.

This changed very rapidly under the twin pressures of a huge influx of European immigrants and the adoption of engineering advances, notably refrigeration. Many of the old-established ales and porters disappeared, as lager beer became the most popular style. Perhaps the most illuminating story is that of the first Milwaukee brewery, which began brewing ale and porter in 1840 under the name of the "Milwaukee Brewery." By 1867, its rivals had already converted to lager, but the Milwaukee Brewery, now called M.

W. Powell & Co., continued until 1880. At this point they abandoned it "because the brewing of ale was less profitable than that of lager beer."

The rest of the story is familiar. Prohibition killed many local American brews, including lagers as well as ales, stouts and porters. A very small number of porters were revived with Repeal, but only Yuengling's version survives today. Sadly, my introduction to the style, Narragansett Porter seems to be no longer available. Perversely, as in England, it is the burgeoning modern micro-breweries and brewpubs which are reviving the porter style.

Porter brewing also spread to other countries, notably Canada where it is still produced by the major brewers. I actually stumbled onto some Labatt's Porter while writing this! It is also produced in Finland, Sweden, Denmark and Russia; I have even sampled a brew under that name in Poland. However, in these countries it does not seem to have been anything more than a niche beer, brewed locally to satisfy a small demand inspired by British exports. As such, there is not a great deal of information to be found on these beers. I didn't even find out much about the Polish version, because I was arrested before I had even finished my first glass. It seems the local police objected to me parking my car in front of their station under a "No Parking" sign! If you are interested in reading more about these beers, Michael Jackson's various writings are the best source, especially his intriguing story of the Le Coq brewery in Estonia.

THE DECLINE OF PORTER

About 1830, a variety of competing pressures combined to decrease porter's popularity. Perhaps the first was technological progress, founded on porter's own success. The London brewers were foremost in the adoption of scientific and engineering advances. They were, for example, the first to install steam engines, with Henry Goodwyn and Whitbread leading the field in 1784, and others soon following. The use of steam and the thermometer enabled them to exert much greater control over the brewing process.

So too did the use of the hydrometer. It did not achieve as rapid an acceptance as may have been expected. James Baverstock, perhaps the first brewer to exploit it, is said to have had to conceal his experiments from his father, who strongly objected to such frivolities. Richardson's publications in the 1780s were crucial in turning the craft of brewing into a science. Before Richardson, only Michael Combrune, describing the use of the thermometer in mashing in his 1762 *Theory and Practice of Brewing*, had published anything quantitative on brewing procedures.

Richardson devised a system of measuring the percentage extract obtained from a given sample of malt. This was to change the character of porter completely, for he showed that brown malt was *not* cheaper than pale malt. When the yield of extract for a given unit cost was taken as the determining factor, rather than the cost per pound of malt, it turned out that pale malt was actually the cheaper of the two. This put brewers on the road to abandoning the use of brown malt.

That did not happen overnight, for one author states that though most of them had given it up by 1819, having turned to a combination of pale and amber malts, Whitbread was still using brown malt at that time. Without it, the brewers had a major problem with obtaining the right color for their porter (a good argument for the beer being translucent and not black). Among techniques used for coloring porter were the addition of burnt sugar and even "burning the sugar of the concentrated wort."

Less savory were the various techniques of adulteration, which were quite widespread in London in the early 19th century, due also in part to cost pressures as the result of increases in the price of malt and hops around 1800. As far as coloring was concerned, licorice and molasses were probably the prime adulterants. However, publications of the period give long lists of other much less desirable substances which found their way into the beer. These included capsicum, ginger, quassia (a bitter substance), coriander, the poisonous berry *Cocculus indicus*, green vitriol (ferrous sulphate), alum and salt, opium, nux vomica (a strychnine-containing extract!), and sulfuric acid, which was supposed to give new porter a mature flavor. These practices must surely have helped lower the reputation of porter in the drinker's eyes and so contributed to its ultimate demise.

Other efforts were being made to develop more suitable coloring agents for porter. One interesting product, patented by a Matthew Wood in 1802, consisted of a wort which had been concentrated to a paste-like consistency. Obviously, this is a kind of malt extract, but the possibilities of actually using such a product as the *main* source of malt in brewing were not considered at that time.

The answer to the whole problem was discovered by Daniel Wheeler, who invented the technique of roasting malt at high temperature (400 degrees F [204.5 degrees C]) to give a highly-colored product. Since he patented his invention in 1817, it was and sometimes still is known as patent malt. Since it was still technically a malt, this product was perfectly acceptable in brewing; its high color meant that it was ideal for the technique of using pale malt to provide extract and small amounts of roast malt to give both color and flavor. This, of course, is exactly the approach practiced in modern brewing.

Patent malt was readily adopted by the brewers. Barclay Perkins was using it by 1820, and Whitbread had tried it in 1817, though they had not completely changed over from brown malt in 1819. In Ireland in 1819, a couple of entrepreneurs set up two malt roasting houses close to Guinness' Dublin brewery. Though we cannot be sure, it seems likely that brown malt (in the original sense) may have ceased to be made not very long after this.

Black malt may have been a double-edged weapon. It may have suited the brewers as a coloring agent, but it probably also altered the flavor of porter somewhat, for it does have a very pronounced burnt flavor. Used in large proportions, it would not only have given a strongly-flavored beer, but one that was black rather than translucent, which we today call dry stout. The term stout was already in use at that time, though perhaps not widely. It was certainly a loose term and may have simply meant any particularly strong beer. So brown stout may have meant nothing more than a premium porter. But with the invention of black malt, stout began to develop as a style in its own right and to put porter another step closer to its demise.

Another pressure on porter was its old rival gin. As I mentioned earlier, by 1830 per capita consumption of the spirit in Britain was close to one gallon per year and had become a severe social problem in London. An 1829 quote from the London newspaper *The Times* ran as follows, "Beer and Porter are the natural beverage of the Englishman...the increase of Gin-drinking and that of suicides, murders, and all kinds of violence are contemporaneous."

Perhaps the worst effect of gin, as far as porter is concerned, was that legislators tried to encourage the drinking of beer instead. One of the ways in which they did this was to introduce in 1830 what became known as the Beerhouse Act. This entitled virtually anyone to retail beer, even from his home, simply by taking out a license costing just two guineas (a little more than two pounds). Up till then, licenses had been controlled by the magistrates, but this Act took that control out of their hands.

Beerhouses proliferated, which must have been a great help to porter's other major competitor, pale ale, since it diluted the tied holdings of the porter brewers and opened more outlets to the provincial pale ale brewers. Further, from 1801 to 1841, the population of London more than doubled. In 1830, the London market made up as much as *one-quarter* of total British beer sales and was, as it had been when porter was first invented, a prime target for provincial brewers.

There appears to have been a change in public taste at that time, and pale ales were growing in popularity. Around 1830, Bass produced only about 11,000 barrels per year. In 1840, Burton was linked to London by rail, and Bass developed even faster than the porter brewers had done in the 18th century. By 1876, it was brewing almost a million barrels per year; Allsopp of Burton was not far behind at 900,000 barrels annually, and both had overtaken the London brewers, which were led by Truman's 600,000 barrels.

Porter did not just slip away, for in 1863 it still made up three-quarters of the beer drunk in London. Charringtons, one of the leading ale brewers in London, actually started brewing porter in 1833. Yet several of the city's porter brewers had been far sighted enough to know that it was on its way out by the 1830s. Whitbread began brewing ale in 1834 and in 1833, according to one report, "Barclay Perkins and other great houses, finding that there is a decrease in the consumption of porter, and an increase in the consumption of ale, have gone into the ale trade; nearly all the new trade is composed of mild ale."

Of course, mild ale did not mean what it means now. Later in the century, Burton mild was actually a stronger beer than the pale ales of the time. The term had been in use for many years. Around 1820, newly-brewed porter was termed mild, and the mild ale of 1833 could have been something similar. Modern dark mild ale certainly seems to have been derived from porter, but its appearance as a definite style is not well documented. Porter was a stock beer, for it was kept at the brewery for long periods before it was sold to the retail trade. Today's mild ale is a running beer, which means that it is shipped out to the customer right away and drunk while still fresh. Perhaps that is how it acquired the name mild, as compared to the designation used for fresh porter.

After 1860, porter's position rapidly eroded, and by 1900 it represented only one-quarter of London's beer consumption. Many of the great porter vats, once the sign of brewing success, were being destroyed at the beginning of this century. Events at Truman, Hanbury, Buxton & Co illustrate this decline nicely. In 1860, ale constituted only one-quarter of the brewery's production, the rest being porter and stout. By 1918, ale represented two-thirds of its total output, and by 1930 the brewing of porter there had ceased entirely.

The public's changing attitude to porter may have come not just from a change in taste, but also from a change in drinking habits. Up until the 19th century, glass was subject to a very high taxation rate and was very expensive. Most pubs would have served beer in pewter and earthenware pots. When this tax was removed in the early 1800s the use of glass became more widespread, and the consumer began to judge beer by its looks as much as by its taste. This is perhaps best summed up by a quote from a statement made to a Parliamentary committee in 1899, "The ordinary customer...is not satisfied with beer unless it is bright and clear, carries a good head and is free from acid. He is not satisfied now with porter in pewter pots, but drinks ale in a glass vessel, the contents of which he can see for himself."

Porter had one more contribution to make in the field of brewing technology. In 1872, Pasteur visited Whitbread's brewery, and inspected a sample of porter under the microscope. He showed that it was significantly infected saying, "This porter leaves much to be desired." His arguments must have been very persuasive, for the brewery staff immediately changed their yeast stock, *and* bought a microscope! This was, of course, four years before Pasteur published his famous book *Etudes sur la biere*.

What appears to have happened is that porter declined in strength, as it also declined in popularity. As far as dark beers were concerned, stout took over the top end of the gravity range. At first, there was no clear distinction between the two beers. In 1854, Flowers of Stratford-upon-Avon was actually advertising a stout porter! Guinness' famous Extra Stout is supposed to have been given that designation to mark its superior quality as compared to plain stout, or plain porter. Many breweries were offering more than one stout, often under the designations single and double, which confuses the picture still further.

In 1843, one writer refers to the "common sort" of porter as having OG 1.050 (12.3 °Plato), while brown stout had OG 1.055 to 1.072 (13.5 to 17.5 °Plato). Rather later (1857) another author quotes common London porter with an OG 1.055 to 1.065 (13.5 to 15.8 °Plato), as compared to ordinary stout brewed at OG 1.073 (17.7 °Plato)! A third author, a Professor Graham, published some very detailed chemical analyses of various British beers in 1880. Unfortunately, he does not list any porters, but he does give some figures for two types of Dublin stout, XX at 1.074 (17.9 °Plato), and XXX at 1.089 (21.3 °Plato).

41

The American authors Wahl & Henius, writing in 1908, give some interesting figures for original gravities of English beers. Porter is the lowest at OG 1.053 to 1.061 (13 to 15 °Plato), single stout is at OG 1.066 to 1.074 (16 to 18 °Plato), double stout at OG 1.074 to 1.083 (18 to 20 °Plato), Imperial stout at OG 1.083 to 1.105 (20 to 25 °Plato), while Russian export is simply quoted as above OG 1.105 (25 °Plato)!

The same authors also quote specifications for American beers, with porter having OG 1.053 (13 °Plato), and stout 1.066 to 1.074 (16 to 18 °Plato), both pretty similar to the figures given for their English-brewed counterparts. Perhaps a more significant point can be gleaned from Wahl & Henius' list of analyses of a wide range of beers from all over the world, carried out from 1879 to 1907. This lists nine different British stouts, two American, one Canadian, and one Swedish porter, but does not include a *single sample of English porter*!

The quality of porter had declined to the extent that it was often the cheapest beer on any brewer's lists. Nithsdale and Manton in *Practical Brewing*, first published in London in 1913, quote the following original gravity specifications: porter 1.040 (9.9 °Plato), mild 1.050 (12.3 °Plato), bitter 1.055 (13.5 °Plato), stout 1.055 (13.5 °Plato). The only beer with lighter gravity than porter was light ale, at OG 1.033 (8.2 °Plato). The other differences between mild and porter were that about 20 percent of the mild grist was made up of sugar, while none was used for the porter, and that the mild was actually more highly hopped!

It is clear from this, and from the fact that much mild is a translucent dark beer, that porter was eventually displaced by mild. As we have seen, English porter disappeared around the 1930s and 1940s. It returned only in 1978 to 1979, thanks to the Penrhos microbrewery and the independent

Timothy Taylor brewery. Porter took longer to die in Ireland, where it finally vanished around 1972. Perhaps the final oddity about porter's involved history is that the dry stout market, which evolved from porter's own almost overwhelming success, should today be dominated in England by Guinness, one of those Irish brewers whose very existence was threatened by imports of London-brewed porter!

2

Profile Of Porter

It is not always a simple matter to precisely define a beer style, particularly a long-established one. There are always ambiguities, especially if it is a widely-brewed beer. We have already seen that this was the case with porter, and there is considerable variety in the modern versions of the style. I have already pointed out that Yuengling's Pottsville Porter is one of the few examples of the style in the English-speaking part of the world that is not a revival. However, this is a bottom-fermented beer and on that account might be considered to be a dark lager, rather than a porter!

Since almost all other versions are revivals, they represent each brewer's opinion of what a porter should be. In some cases, original recipes have been adapted to modern raw materials; in others, the brewers have created their own recipes from scratch. Brewers, and particularly microbrewers, are individualistic people, so it is not surprising that their beers do not always fit into clearly-defined niches. For example, I would define some modern porters as really being stouts, although others would say that if the brewer calls it porter, that is exactly what it is!

There are actually only around 30 versions of porter

Label courtesy of American
Breweriana Association.

produced in the United States and Britain, and they do
cover a fair range of original gravities and colors. There are
only two that purport to be London porters, which should,
after all, be the standard. These are the Pitfield Brewery's
London Porter, now brewed in the Midlands, and the Orange Brewery's Pimlico Porter, produced at a brewpub close
to the Westminster area of London.

London Porter is brewed to an adaptation of an old
Whitbread recipe, which should make it fairly authentic! It
has an OG 1.058 (14.2 °Plato) and a very deep color, just
barely translucent in a half-pint glass. Pimlico Porter, on the
other hand, is not so strong, with OG 1.046 (11.3 °Plato) and,
although still a dark beer, is considerably more translucent
than the Pitfield beer. The latter's bitter flavor seems to
come more from roasted malt than from the hops, while the
reverse is true of Pimlico porter. However, both are excellent
beers, and both have a smoothness and easy drinkability,
which I believe is an important characteristic of porter.

I am not going to list the contradictions of other present-day porters, since that would simply be confusing. Instead, I am going to give my opinion as to what the beer's profile should be. In fact, it is not going to be too personal a definition, for I shall found it on the knowledge we developed in the previous section. Actually, it is not so difficult to define porter after all. There are no longer many dark top-fermented beers, and the only one with which porter can really be confused is stout. Fortunately, that is now a clearly-defined style, so it is fairly simple to make a distinction between the two beers. I shall discuss that a bit further later on.

PORTER

Original Specific Gravity: 1.045 to 1.060 (11 to 14.7 °Plato)
Apparent Final Gravity: 1.010 to 1.015 (2.5 to 3.8 °Plato)
Apparent Degree of Attenuation: 75 to 80 percent
Real Degree of Attenuation: 55 to 65 percent
Reducing Sugars (as maltose): 1 to 2 percent
Acidity (as lactic acid): 0.2 percent
pH: 3.9 to 4.4
Color: 35 to 70 °L
Bitterness: 7 to 12 HBU/five gallons; 25 to 45 IBU
Alcohol: 3.6 to 4.8 percent w/w; 4.5 to 5.5 percent v/v

This is obviously a fairly broad specification, which is quite deliberate. You *have* a good deal of elbow room when it comes to designing porter, particularly when it comes to starting gravity and color, and it is these two which really determine the precise level of bittering required. I am going to discuss these in more detail in the following section on aroma and flavor. The cynics among you will have noticed that much of the above profile is not very different for the one given for pale ale, in the first book of this series. This is neither accident nor laziness on my part. It is more a reflection on the difficulty of defining a beer style by purely physico-chemical methods, and also points up the fact that there *will* be a good many similarities between top-fermented beers by definition. The key difference between the two is that of color, because the addition of roasted malts to give porter its characteristic color is what determines that its flavor will be very different from that of pale ale.

It is also important to consider carbonation levels. I have not done so above, for it depends on whether you view porter as being a real draught ale (as was the original) or as a bottled beer. As a beer stored for many months, porter would not have been at all heavily carbonated, for the wooden vats in which it was stored were porous, so that it would have gradually lost carbonation over time. The modern English forms are mostly real draught beers, and so are low in carbonation (0.75 to 1 volumes). Some are bottled, as are many of the American versions, and in this form they are often much more highly carbonated (up to 2.5 volumes). Although I am firmly convinced that excessive carbonation spoils any beer, the pronounced flavor of porter can take higher carbonation levels than, for example, pale ale. But please do not overdo it, it is a beer of great complexity, and too much gas will simply overwhelm it!

AROMA AND FLAVOR OF PORTER

I think the first point here is that porter should have a full-bodied malty flavor. A good deal of that should come from the roasted and caramel malts used to color and flavor it, but some too must come from the pale malt base and the unfermented dextrins arising from the mashing of the pale malt. It is also a beer that needs a reasonable alcohol content to give it the desired level of warmth and balance.

Therefore, the original gravity should not be too low. Yet at least 10 of Britain's modern porters do not fit my minimum, for they lie between OG 1.040 to 1.045 (9.9 to 11.1 °Plato). Of course, my figures are only guidelines, and you can go lower if you wish. However, at low original gravities it is very easy to get the beer out of balance and have the roasted malt flavors and/or hop bitterness stand out too distinctly. My personal preference is for the fairly narrow OG range of 1.050 to 1.055 (12.3 to 13.5 °Plato). You can, according to your taste, go much higher, up to OG 1.070 (17.0 °Plato) or more, but you then run the risk of giving the beer too much estery, barley-wine flavor.

Porter, as would befit a long-stored beer, should be fairly well attenuated, the finishing gravity being about one-quarter original gravity or a little less. In other words, it should be dry, and certainly not noticeably sweet. It should have a definite but not marked estery character, and the burnt, coffee-like taste of roasted malt, topped off by a definite hop bitterness and a good heavy fullness, or mouth-feel. Above all, this spectrum of flavors should be balanced.

What does balanced really mean? It is a term which is often used by brewers and writers, but seldom explained. That is partly because it is a term which is not easy to explain, although it may be quite obvious when a particular beer is tasted. My explanation of the term is that a balanced beer is one in which all the flavor notes contribute without any one of them being noticeably dominant. In other words, the taste of the beer is experienced almost as if it were one complete flavor.

Please do not confuse balanced and bland. A bland beer drinks smoothly with no separate flavors, because it has very little flavor anyway! A balanced beer, on the other hand, can have many very definite flavors, but these tend to merge and complement each other, rather than standing out as separate sensations.

Naturally, since different flavors are perceived on different parts of the tongue, even in a balanced beer they can be separately picked out by careful tasting. This is particularly true of bitterness, which tends to be the last flavor experienced, since it is detected on the back of the tongue. However, even though the profile gives fairly high levels of bitterness, in a porter these tend to be matched by and mingle with the aromatic flavors from the roasted malts. Such hop levels in a pale ale result in a beer whose *main* flavor note is hop bitterness, but this should not be the case with porter. If you find that it is, then reduce your hopping rates accordingly.

One last point on this question of balance. It is my view that if your porter does have a pronounced hop bitterness *and* a strong roast malt flavor, which readily come through as separate components, then it is not a porter at all. It is, by definition, a dry stout instead! I said that this had become a clearly-defined style, and those are the most important aspects of the flavor spectrum of a modern dry stout.

The aroma of porter is also important, though it should rarely be overwhelming. There should be malty, grainy notes and some hints of fruit from the esters, along with the burnt, pungent, even slightly phenolic notes from the roast malt. Hop aroma, though probably not present in the original version, is not out of place either, though it should not be overdone. Indeed, very many of the new American porters use aroma hops, including some of the more strongly-flavored varieties, such as Northern Brewer, as well as the more traditional aroma varieties such as Goldings, Hallertauer and Cascade.

Finally, we have to discuss color. You might wonder why a visual attribute should be considered along with flavor and aroma, from which it is ordinarily quite separate. In fact, all three are inseparably linked in the case of a beer such as porter. This is because the dark color of porter comes from roasted malts, and the flavor and aroma characteristics vary quite widely. There are three types to choose from: chocolate malt, black malt and roasted barley.

We shall discuss these in more detail under the section on ingredients, but they do warrant some consideration here. Although some color will come from the pale and crystal malts, the deep-brown to black color of porter is imparted by the use of one or more of these three.

I have repeated many times that porter should be a translucent beer, with a deep ruby shade, perhaps very dark brown rather than black overall. Of course, this is a little subjective, and it depends how you determine the color. I have given a range for °L in the profile, but physical methods can be misleading in the case of dark beers. I like to evaluate my porter by eye, using a straight pint glass, or "sleeve," held up to the light. If I can *just* see through the glass and pick out definite red hints, then I am happy. Perhaps a more reliable method is to use a conical pilsener glass, in which the beer will appear much more translucent. If you are not sure about this, buy samples of the various commercial porters and try each one by either or both methods. Concentrate on the differences in color, rather than the similarities, and you will soon learn what to look for in your own beers.

We have seen that black malt goes back nearly 200 years as a coloring agent for porter, so it is perhaps the most authentic of the three in the absence of the original brown malt. However, it does have quite a bitter aromatic character and can easily make the beer taste unbalanced, and more like a dry stout. It also tends to give the beer a black, rather than red-brown hue. Roasted barley is somewhat less aromatic, but can be more bitter than black malt, yields a black-brown color, and is ideally suited for the brewing of dry stouts. Chocolate malt, on the other hand, has a much softer, less burnt and gentler aromatic character than the other two and does lend the beer a more desirable reddish shade.

All three types are used by modern porter brewers, with black malt seemingly more popular in America, while chocolate gets the vote in Britain. The American Homebrewers Association, in its specifications for entries in the 1991 National Homebrew Competition deems it necessary to define *two* types of porter. The first is "Robust Porter," with the accent on black malt flavor and *no* roast barley character; the second is "Brown Porter," with no roast barley *or* strong burnt malt character. Personally, I would prefer to think of porter as one beer with a whole continuum of roasted malt flavors.

I think this apparent confusion over which is the roasted malt most suited to this style simply emphasizes that although porter may be a balanced beer, it is still a brew of infinite and highly variable complexity. It is therefore a fertile field for the imaginative brewer to work and offers you many possibilities for devising your own version of a historic brew.

3

Porter Brewing - Raw Materials And Equipment

INGREDIENTS

- Malt -

Pale Malt. As we have seen, this is the base of porter, contributing the bulk of fermentable material, as well as some of the "body-building" dextrins. Apart from the latter, its contribution to flavor is much smaller than would be the case in a pale beer. Therefore, even though this is really an English beer, we are not restricted to using only English pale malt, though this does indeed work well for porter.

English pale malt comes from two-row barley, is well-modified, and is relatively low in nitrogen. For a full explanation of these terms, see *Pale Ale*, in the *Classic Beer Style Series* from Brewers Publications. Briefly, it means that the malt is relatively highly colored (about 3°L) and contains only a moderate amount of starch-degrading enzymes, but it is low in protein (around 1 1/2 percent nitrogen). It is therefore ideally suited to mashing by single-stage infusion at about 150 degrees F (65.5 degrees C), which is the so-called saccharification temperature.

American pale malt comes from either two-row or six-row barley, with the latter being the most common. Both are paler than the British type (1.4 to 1.9° L), higher in nitrogen (around 2 percent), and higher in enzyme content. Normal brewing practice requires a protein rest at around 122 degrees F (50 degrees C), before the saccharification stage. The purpose of this is both to liberate starch from the protein matrix, so as to ensure good yield of extract, and to degrade high molecular weight proteins which might otherwise cause chill haze in refrigerated beers.

In fact, in the case of porter this step may not be necessary. My preference is to include the protein rest, since I find it gives me better control over the brewing process and more reproducible results. But most modern U.S. malts are modified enough to give good yields of extract in a single-temperature infusion mash, and chill haze is not a serious problem in a fairly dark beer, which should *not* be served cold. It is your choice, for there are some excellent porters brewed from American malt by single-stage infusion.

The six-row malts are really designed for lager brewing, and with their high enzyme content, specifically for the high-adjunct pale American pilseners. They have, in fact, a grainy, rather than a malty flavor, in contrast to the two-row variety. As a result, the latter is generally preferred for a beer such as porter. Klages is one of the best known two-row malts and is readily available from homebrewing suppliers.

I would recommend that if you are new to porter brewing, particularly if you are inexperienced at mashing, that you stick with British pale malt. It is simpler to handle, including grinding as well as mashing, and I think it does add something to the flavor of a porter, which American malt does not. However, since pale malt contributes only slightly to porter flavor, this may simply be a case of heredity overcoming objectivity!

Typical extract figures for British and Klages pale malt are about the same, around 80 percent. This means that the maximum yield you can expect to get is 36 °/pound/gallon (that is, one pound of malt will give one gallon of wort, OG 1.036). There is little difference in the cost as far as most homebrewers are concerned. American six-row pale malt is often cheaper than either of these, but commonly gives a little lower yield, about 78 percent extract, or 34 °/pound/ gallon. In practice, most homebrewers will not do any better than 30 to 31 °/pound/gallon, and this should be borne in mind when formulating recipes.

Crystal Malt. This is a malt which has a very important part to play in the production of porter. As a roasted malt, it contains no enzymes and no starch, although it does make a significant contribution to extract. In fact, it is "stewed" rather than roasted, since it is green malt taken to high temperatures under conditions where much of its moisture is retained. As a result, the starch is largely converted to sugars, some of which are caramelised in the process. It does not need mashing, for all of its qualities can be leached out with hot water. It is a malt that the extract, as well as the mashing, brewer will need to use.

Crystal malt can provide a slightly sweet, luscious note, body or mouthfeel, and color to the brew. It is particularly useful in porter for both mouthfeel and color, and contributes significantly to the red hue I have talked so much about. Indeed, I think this is really the clue to bridging the gap between the original porter brewed from brown malt, and the colorized version brewed from pale and roast malts. Its lusciousness nicely links the background maltiness from the pale malt with the stronger flavors of black or chocolate malt, helping to ensure balance rather than contrast.

It can easily be overdone. When I first came to this country and saw that U.S. crystal malts were less caramelised than the British versions I was used to, I thought this offered me a way to re-create the original porter style by matching brown malt with an equal mixture of pale and crystal malts. That beer is seven or eight years old now, with a very pronounced, biting flavor which has not moderated at all with maturation!

There are a variety of crystal malts available, varying in the proportion of caramel and color (up to 90 to 100 °L). Since it is both caramel and color which we are looking for in porter, it is the most highly-roasted versions that we want. For the home brewer, this means that you should go with British crystal malt, which is readily available.

Unlike the case with pale beers, crystal malt can be added in significant amounts to a porter, forming up to about 10 percent of the total weight of the grist. Exactly how much depends upon which of the three dark malts you decide to use. In a pale beer, crystal malt has a profound effect on absolute levels of color, but in porter it tends to effect the shade, rather than the depth. Bear this in mind if you are trying to calculate the final color from the color of the malts used, as in the method described by Byron Burch (*Beer and Brewing, Vol. 7*, pp. 21 to 37, Brewers Publications, 1987). Remember also that crystal malt in these quantities will increase extract, and therefore wort gravity. It commonly has an extract of 60 to 65 percent, and for most homebrewers will yield around 25 °/pound/gallon.

Malt Extract. If you do not mash, then this is the alternative as the main source of extract. It is difficult to be precise in discussing these, since they come in a great variety. Some come as straight malt extracts, some as pre-hopped extracts, and some as kits designed to produce a particular style of beer. All are proprietary products, and the vast majority are British in origin, although American, Canadian, Australian and German are also available.

Label courtesy of American Breweriana Association.

The better extracts are often produced to match particular beer styles, both pale and dark. Those intended for any type of lager are probably not suitable for a beer like porter, whereas those designed for brewing almost any kind of ale, or even stout, can be used as a good porter base. However, if it is meant for a dark beer, you have already lost control over the final color, particularly if the manufacturer has used black malt, and you prefer the flavor of chocolate.

The problem with extracts is that you do not always know exactly what has gone into them, so that it is difficult to decide what adjustments to make to produce the particular flavor range you want. Some of the better suppliers will give you a reasonable description of their extracts, and articles in *zymurgy* (Special Issue 1986, Vol. 9, No. 4, pp. 22 to 23; Winter 1985, Vol. 8, No. 5, pp. 30 to 31; Spring 1986, Vol. 9, No. 1, p. 22) are often a good source of information.

No extracts are specifically designed for porter brewing, as far as I am aware. Therefore, whichever one you opt for, you are also going to have to use some crystal, and one or more of the dark roasted malts. You will probably want to use some aroma hops and will almost certainly want to aim

57

for a higher hop bitterness level than you will get from most pre-hopped extracts. All of which suggests that your best approach is to use a plain, unhopped pale extract, preferably one intended for pale ale or bitter production.

I do not want to put you off using extract. Since so much of the flavor comes from the hops and roasted malts, it is a relatively simple matter to brew excellent porters from malt extract. All I am trying to do is to persuade you to give yourself room to maneuver, so that you can turn out something which is truly your own version of porter.

Most extracts will give you a yield of around 36 °/pound/ gallon. Many of them are highly fermentable and tend to give a thin beer. If you find that to be the case, then you may want to use the partial mash technique. This involves carrying out a simple infusion mash with one to two pounds pale malt, adding the resultant wort to your brewing liquor as you dissolve up the extract. It is a way to give the beer a little extra body and is often worthwhile with porters at the lower end of the recommended gravity range. I shall deal with this further in the section on recipes.

Chocolate Malt. I have already spent some time on the importance of this and the other dark roast malts in giving porter its characteristic color and flavor. It is my personal choice for a porter, since it does give a redder hue to the beer, and its roasted flavor is softer, more rounded and less pronounced than that of black malt. I think it is easier to achieve the balance which is so important in a porter with this malt, than with black malt or roasted barley.

It is produced by roasting malt at temperatures up to 450 degrees F (232 degrees C), which causes some complicated chemical reactions to occur, resulting in significant weight loss. The grains remain intact but have a typical dark brown color from which the name is derived. It has a color of 325 to 375 °L, and about 60 to 65 percent extract (about

20 to 25 °/pound/gallon). Chocolate malt does, of course, contain no enzymes and does not need mashing. If you are brewing from malt extract, everything you want can be obtained by leaching it with hot water. In a full-mash beer it is ground and mashed along with the pale and crystal malts.

The extract yield, though perhaps important to a commercial brewer, is not really significant for relatively small amounts are used in a beer such as porter. It depends on how deep you want the color, and what kind of hop bittering level you have aimed for, but you are likely to use no more than one-half pound of chocolate malt in a five gallon batch.

Black Malt. This malt is prepared in an almost identical manner to chocolate malt, but the roasting is taken just a little further, so that it is higher in color: 475 to 525 °L. As you might expect from its name, the finished product certainly looks much blacker than chocolate malt. But the extra roasting results in more than just a darker color, for other reactions seem to have taken place, so that, in my opinion it has a harsher, more aromatic, even acrid flavor. I emphasize again that this malt can easily take a porter over the top, making it unbalanced and closer to a dry stout.

Black malt will yield about the same amount of extract as chocolate malt and is used in the same way. Again, the actual amount you are likely to use depends upon a number of factors, but I consider four to six ounces in a five gallon batch is probably enough in most cases. If you like the flavor, but do not want to overdo it, then you can advantageously mix a little with chocolate malt to get the best of both worlds.

Roasted Barley. This, as its name indicates, is raw barley which has been roasted in the same way as black and chocolate malts. However, since the starting material is quite different, the finished product is also significantly different from the other roasted malts. It gives about the same yield of extract and is used in exactly the same way as black or chocolate malt.

Roasted barley has a slightly higher color than black malt, 500 to 525 °L, with a definite black rather than black-brown shade. It has a drier, sharper flavor than black malt, which is why it is most suited to the brewing of dry stouts, and why it can easily put a porter out of balance. I really do not like it in a porter, unless used in combination with chocolate malt, or perhaps in a brew with a very high level of hop bitterness. I would certainly limit it to a maximum of four ounces per five gallon brew; many people might find even that amount excessive.

Wheat Malt. This product, either in the form of grain or as wheat flour, is quite popular with English commercial brewers and is often included in porter grists. The main reason for doing so, since it does not add much to color, body or flavor in a beer dominated by roast malts, is that it does improve head retention.

To my mind, brewers who use it in a beer such as porter have simply followed a trend and are not really thinking clearly about the kind of beer they are brewing. An additive which improves head retention without much affect on color is desirable in a low-gravity pale pilsener or light ale, particularly if high levels of adjuncts such as rice or corn are used. With a high gravity beer like porter, brewed with a significant proportion of roasted malts, there will be no lack of head retention, so there should be no need to incorporate wheat malt into the grist.

There is one case where you might want to add wheat malt, and that is when a substantial part of the pale or roasted malts is to be replaced with sugar. This dilutes the malt protein degradation products which are largely responsible for inhibiting the breaking of the bubbles which form the head, so that it collapses soon after formation. If you want to make a beer this way, include a small amount of wheat malt in the grist (up to about 1 to 2 percent, or around four ounces per five gallon brew), and you will find it will hold its head quite well. Whether it is desirable to brew porter from a high-sugar grist is another question, which I shall discuss next.

Sugar. I have gone on record on many occasions as saying sugar has no place in the arsenal of the brewer of quality beers, except for priming purposes. I stand by those statements, but would point out that what I meant was that the use of corn or cane sugar as a *substitute* for malt would result in a thin, alcoholic and unappetizing beer.

It is actually possible to use sugar as a flavoring, when it is unrefined, and when it is used as a true additive, rather than as a substitute. Some brewers favor the use of brown sugar, the very dark muscovado sugar, or even molasses in porter brewing, and we have seen that the latter was widely used in American commercial brewing in the last century.

I would not discourage you from experimenting with these sugars, although I do not favor their use. My own experience is that you have to use fairly large amounts, up to one pound/five gallons or more, to substantially affect final beer flavor. If you do that, then you will increase alcohol content significantly, since even raw sugars are almost totally fermentable by yeast, without adding anything to the beer's body. That means it will taste thinner, and if you have used a lot of hops, or a lot of roasted malt, it will be way out of balance.

It seems to me that this is an unnecessary complication. To brew porter successfully, you must achieve a balance. And the spectrum of porter's flavor has to be made up from a palette consisting of the contributions from pale malt, crystal malt, hops, and one or more of the dark roasted malts. That is a lot of variables to permute, so why put another one into the equation, when its positive contribution can only be a small one?

Flaked Maize. This is widely used in British brewing as a so-called nitrogen diluent, and therefore as a reducer of chill haze. A number of the new English porters include it in their grist, but this is really "whistling in the wind." With a dark beer, served at cellar temperature rather than cold, chill haze should not be a problem. With the high gravity of this beer, flaked maize will have little positive effect, unless used to such an extent that it dilutes and unbalances the flavor. Include it if you wish, but my advice is to avoid it.

Flaked Barley. Here we have a product that is widely used in the brewing of dry stout, largely for its excellent head retention properties, since the formation of a tight, long-lasting head is an important characteristic of this style of beer. It could also be used to advantage in porters, for it is a source of extract and therefore body, as well as head retention.

Flaked barley will yield about 70 percent extract, or around 30 °/pound/gallon. As a source of starch, it will add both fermentable sugars and body to the brew, but little in the way of color. It must be mashed to properly obtain its full benefits. These are perhaps not required in a full grain-mash brew, where lack of head retention is rarely a problem, except at very high original gravities and high alcohol contents.

However, flaked barley can be a very useful adjunct in malt extract beers, which sometimes show poor head retention properties. Like wheat malt, flaked barley can also help high-sugar beers to hold a head better. Indeed, I think it is somewhat superior to wheat malt for this purpose. If you wish to include it in your brew, you *must* do so in a partial mash with pale malt, since the flaked barley is low in starch-degrading enzymes. For a final brew length of five gallons use about one-half pound flaked barley, along with the desired amount and type of roasted and crystal malts, and one to two pounds pale malt in the partial mash.

- Hops -

In any beer worth the name, this is a very important raw material. The predominant hop characteristic in a beer is bitterness, but this unusual plant can also add aromatic flavor and aroma notes depending upon the way it is used. All three of these hop characters make their contribution to the magic of porter. It is important to remember that though its flavor is balanced, it is a complex beer, and hop bitterness and character are a part of its complexity.

Hop aroma can come from late hopping during or at the end of the boil, or by dry hopping during fermentation, or at the final kegging or casking. Only the freshest hops should be used at these stages, or off-flavors will result. Just remember, if hop character and/or aroma are overdone, the beer will lose its balance.

Almost any bittering hop will do for porter, so long as it is in good condition and not stale. Goldings are the classic high-quality English hop, but as already pointed out, they were not used in the original porters. In fact, it is probable that the slightly coarser types, in the style of Fuggle, were more commonly used for this type of beer. Some excellent porters are produced both here and in England that use high alpha acid hops such as Galena, Eroica, Talisman, Cluster, Chinook, Target and Challenger. Curiously, few seem to use Northern Brewer, which would appear to be admirably suited for this purpose.

Northern Brewer, on the other hand, is used as an

aroma hop by some American brewers. It has what is some-times described as a black currant flavor, which can be objectionable in a pale beer, but which mixes well in the complexity of porter. Other popular aroma hops are Goldings and Hallertauer (both of which are classics for any style of beer), Cascades, Fuggle and Chinook.

I think this simply underlines that you can go with almost any variety for either bittering or aroma, so long as it fits with the flavors from the various malts to result in a balance (sorry to keep using that word!). My own preferred approach is to use any high alpha acid variety (that is 7 percent alpha and above) for bittering and to stick with the classic aromatic varieties, such as Goldings, Hallertauer and Cascade, for late or dry-hopping.

A further question about hops is whether pellets are better than the loose or leaf form. As far as bitterness goes pellets are probably better, in so far as they are more uniform, so that you can readily achieve reproducible levels of bitter-ness. It may be a different story when it comes to aroma.

Some heat is evolved during the pelletisation process, and this can result in the loss of part of the essential oils which are the source of hop aroma. However, if the process is carefully done, such loss should be small. Moreover, pellet hops are often carefully packed and sealed under nitrogen, which prevents further loss or oxidation of oils. Leaf hops are often not stored as well, and unless in good condition, they may have lost a significant proportion of the aroma-yielding oils.

Generally, I prefer loose hops for aroma purposes, especially dry hopping. I think that at their best such hops will give a fragrance to the aroma of the beer that is difficult to achieve with pellets of the same variety. However, I have had acceptable results with pellets, and they are certainly more convenient to use, particularly if you want to add aroma hops during fermentation.

Which type you choose will depend on your supplier. Many of them take great care with both loose and pellet hops these days, but you cannot always be sure what happened to the leaf hops *before* they reached the supplier, especially if they are imported varieties. Actual appearances can be misleading, and the best way to test leaf hops is to rub a few in your hands, so as to liberate the yellow hop resins, and smell them. If they have a fine, clean and fragrant odor, use them; if they smell at all rancid, or if the odor is one you would not like your beer to have, use pellets instead.

I am not going to suggest here that any particular varieties should be used in porters, either for bittering or aroma. Specific varieties will be recommended in the recipe section, but these recommendations are not intended to be exclusive. With the exception of a few English high-alpha varieties, such as Northdown, almost all the commercially grown varieties, including new and even experimental ones, are available from homebrewing suppliers. There is such a range of them, particularly when it comes to aroma hops, that we are spoiled for choice. I would encourage you to experiment with all of them and select the varieties which best suit your own taste.

Let me just point out that my own approach is pretty much that followed by commercial brewers, with the high-alpha varieties being used for bittering, and the aroma hops chosen only for their aroma and used regardless of their alpha acid content. In the first book of this series (*Pale Ale, Classic Beer Style Series*, p. 50, Brewers Publications, 1990) you will find a listing of the properties of most of the commonly available varieties. The better suppliers also offer a good deal of information about the varieties they sell, which should help you in making your choice.

I think it useful at this point to consider what is meant by the terms Homebrew Bitterness Units (HBU), and Inter-

Label courtesy of American
Breweriana Association.

national Bittering Units (IBU), just so there is no confusion in understanding the recipes. HBU is the weight (in ounces) of hops used, multiplied by their alpha acid percentage. Therefore, if you add two ounces of Northern Brewer, at 10 percent alpha acid, you have 20 HBU. Conversely, if you want to use Goldings at 4 percent alpha acid to achieve 20 HBU, you will need five ounces.

The difficulty with HBU is that it is just a number and is only meaningful when related to the brew length. In other words, you must say 20 HBU in five gallons. That means for a similar bittering effect, you need 40 HBU for a 10 gallon brew length. What is more, HBU does not tell you anything about the level of bittering in a beer, since it is a measure of what you put in, not what you get out!

A good deal of the alpha acid added to the boil is either not extracted or lost at other stages of brewing, such as with the trub or during fermentation. Even the most efficient commercial brewers do not expect to achieve better than 35 percent utilization of alpha acids added to the copper, particularly if they are not added at the start of the boil. Microbrewers and homebrewers can expect to get a lower utilization.

I cannot tell you what this should be in any particular case, since it depends on the precise details of your brewing process. Microbrewers would be well-advised to determine their utilization rates by having representative beers analyzed for IBU and calculating back from the added alpha acids. In the case of homebrewers, you probably will not do much better than 25 percent, which is the figure I have used in calculating IBUs for the beers in the recipe section. Malt extract brewers who use only a portion of their brew length in the boil, and therefore have a fairly concentrated wort, may get even lower utilization rates.

In contrast to HBU, IBU is an actual analytical figure, determined by an internationally accepted method. It is the concentration of iso-alpha-acids in the finished beer in units of milligrams per liter (mg/L). IBU is the best guide to how bitter a beer actually tastes, because iso-alpha acids are the true bittering substances in beer; they are derived from alpha acids by reactions occurring during wort boiling.

There is an approximate relation between HBU and IBU, providing the utilization rate is known. If this is assumed to be 25 percent, and the brew length is five gallons, then:

$$IBU = \frac{(HBU) \times 28.4 \times 1000 \times 0.25}{100 \times 3.78 \times 5}$$

Do not worry too much about the actual numbers, they are simply there to convert "ounces per five gallons" into mg/L. A simpler form of the equation is:

$$IBU = 3.76 \times HBU$$

Of course, if you use a different brew length, you will have to substitute that for "5" in the first equation and recalculate the constant in the second equation.

You may think this is an unnecessary complication for an average homebrewer. Actually, I have kept it quite simple. Byron Burch (*Brewing Quality Beers*, pp. 56 to 59, Joby Books, 1986) goes into this in greater depth, making allowances for multiple hop additions at different times during the boil.

You may not want to go that far, but you certainly should at least use one of the above equations to obtain an approximate idea of the IBU level in your beer. How else are you going to match any beer style, including porter, since these are always defined in terms of IBU, for commercial brewers do not use HBU!

- Yeast -

I have pointed out that some commercial porters, including a few with a long pedigree, are brewed with bottom-fermenting yeasts. The original and most modern versions use top-fermenting yeasts. It can therefore be argued that either type of yeast is suited to the brewing of this beer. However, I think that there is little doubt that porter is at its best when one of its flavor aspects is a fruitiness due to the presence of esters. Bottom-fermenting yeasts in general produce very low levels of esters, which is partly why lager beers have a cleaner, smoother flavor than do most ales. Top yeasts, on the other hand, normally produce relatively high levels of esters. On this ground alone, top-fermenting yeasts are the first choice for making porter.

Of course, ester formation is a function of temperature, as well as yeast type. For a given yeast strain more esters will be produced as the fermentation temperature increases. Up to a point that is fine, since top-fermenting yeasts perform more efficiently at higher temperatures, ensuring the good attenuation needed in this style of beer. However, do not get carried away, for too high a temperature will produce, among other things, a very high level of esters. Fermentations above, say 75 to 80 degrees F (24 to 27 degrees C) will result in a very high level of esters, which will not only throw the beer's flavor out of balance, but will also often make it actually unpleasant.

One other thing we want from our porter yeast is good attenuation, so that the beer does not have too much residual sweetness. It is important that fermentation goes close to completion in the primary, and if necessary it should continue in the secondary fermentation/maturation step. With top-fermenting yeasts, this will not happen if the yeast is highly flocculent, that is if it tends to clump together and settle out rapidly. Be careful though, some yeasts (known as powdery yeasts) give excellent attenuation because they stay in suspension forever, and it is very difficult to get the beer to clarify. What we want is something in between, giving good attentuation, but flocculating and settling out well once its job is done.

In short, what the porter brewer needs is a medium flocculent, well-attenuating ale yeast. Preferably, it should be one that is used to a similar environment, but that is obviously going to be difficult to find nowadays. English ale yeasts are the most suitable for our purposes, while those used for moderately strong dry stout would be the best. For microbrewers, some experimentation is probably necessary, since the choice of yeast is partly dictated by the other flavor components present in your chosen version of porter. If you are already brewing other styles of beers and want to keep to the same strain of yeast to prevent the risk of cross-contamination, that is fine so long as it can handle the attenuation. But you may have to adjust hopping rates and levels of roast malts to balance that yeast's flavor profile in terms of both attenuation and ester production.

For the homebrewer, there may not be a lot of choice. We have not yet come up with a proper solution to the problem of providing the occasional brewer with a variety of suitable yeasts with a large enough number of active cells to handle fermentation of a five gallon brew, and at a reasonable cost. The biggest difficulty is that even a yeast of the right type needs to be pitched in sufficient quantity to handle the brew length, which is about two million *active* cells per milliliter! If you do not have that much, then fermentation will be slow to start with a consequent risk of infection, and attenuation may suffer because the yeast is just outnumbered and struggling all the time.

One way around that, whatever your choice of yeast, is to make a starter. For best results, you have to make a small starter to begin with (around one-half pint of wort), then keep doubling its volume as the yeast becomes fully active, until you have one-half gallon of vigorously fermenting starter to pitch into your five gallons of wort. This is not an easy technique. The first problem is timing, since you have to get the starter going several days before the wort is ready. The whole effort is pretty pointless if the cooled wort has to sit around waiting for the starter to get properly going! The second problem is that there is a big risk of introducing bacterial and wild yeast contamination in preparing a starter, and you hardly want to add an active infecting culture to your newly-brewed beer!

Nevertheless, I do recommend that you seriously consider making a starter. Once you learn to do it properly, you will find the results well worth it. Do not just take my word for it, read what Paul Farnsworth has to say about it in *Beer and Brewing*, (Vol. 9, pp. 67 to 85, Brewers Publications, 1989) as well as the *zymurgy* issue on yeast (Special Issue 1989, Vol. 12, No. 4), and Rodney Morris (*zymurgy*, Spring 1991, Vol. 14, No. 1, pp. 31 to 33).

As to selection of a particular strain of yeast, many retailers stock a number of dried and liquid culture yeasts these days. Dried yeasts have been the standby of the homebrewer for many years. In the past, they have often been of dubious quality, sometimes not true brewing yeasts and sometimes highly infected. In general, the quality of these yeasts has improved dramatically, but there is still a risk of contaminating your beer, especially if the yeast has not been properly stored, or is not fresh. The only spoiled brew I have had in many years was a few months ago, when I mistakenly used a sample of dried yeast I had kept for a couple of years!

There are several brand name dried yeasts and a few named strains. Notable among these is a Whitbread Ale Yeast. Bearing in mind Whitbread's part in the porter story, you may well consider trying this particular yeast. It is not, of course, an authentic porter yeast, but it is a good ale yeast, which is what you are after. Almost any of the other varieties of ale yeast on the market should also give acceptable results.

The liquid cultures available are often high quality yeasts, and several of them are ale yeasts which are suitable for porter fermentations. They are somewhat more expensive than dried yeast, but not prohibitively so. The problem with liquid yeasts is that they are killed on storage much more readily than dried yeasts, so that if you use them as recommended, you may again be under-pitching the wort.

These yeasts are unlikely to carry contaminating bacteria or wild yeasts, whereas some contamination is almost inevitable with dried yeasts due to the processing method. However, if they are mostly dead when you pitch them, fermentation will be very slow in commencing, and your will likely pick up infecting organisms from the atmosphere anyway. This means that it is almost always preferable to make a starter from the culture.

One company has got around the risk of introducing infection in making a starter by packing the culture in a pouch which contains a second pack of yeast nutrient. To use it, you simply bang the pouch to break the nutrient pack, give it a few days to ferment and swell the pouch, then add it to your wort. There are two problems with this, the first being that of timing, for the period it takes to reach a fully active state will depend on how much of the yeast has died during storage and transport. The second is that even when fully active, there still is not really a sufficient quantity of yeast in one pouch to handle a full five gallons of wort.

The real answer, of course, is to learn how to handle yeast, so that you can not only make clean, vigorous starters, but can also prepare your own cultures. This way, you can build up your own bank of yeast strains, and be sure that you have exactly the right one handy whenever you need it. This takes some care and a good deal of time, but the results are well worth it. I cannot go into the details of culturing here, but there is plenty of information on it in the homebrewing literature; a good place to start is the *zymurgy* special issue on yeast.

◄ Water ►

Since part of the reason for porter's origin in London was that the water supply there was peculiarly suited for the brewing of dark beers, you will probably want to consider matching its quality in brewing your own porter. This is actually a very difficult thing to do with any precision, unless you are prepared to strip out all the dissolved ions by cation/anion exchange resins, and then rebuild the water by the addition of the appropriate amounts of the required mineral salts. I am only going to touch lightly upon water treatment here. If you wish to know more about the subject, read Gregory Noonan's *Brewing Lager Beer* (Brewers Publications, 1986), *Malting and Brewing Science* by J. S. Hough, D. E. Briggs, R. Stevens and T. W. Young (Chapman and Hall, 1982), or Darryl Richman's article "Water Treatment: How to Calculate Salt Adjustment" (*zymurgy* Winter 1989, Vol. 12, No. 5).

We now know that there were sound chemical reasons as to why water from a particular area was suitable for brewing only certain specific beer styles. Mainly, though this is something of a simplification, it was a question of achieving the correct acidity in mashing. The mash should have pH 5.0 to 5.5 to permit optimum malt enzyme activity, and therefore maximum conversion of starch into fermentable extract.

If the water is high in carbonate, this is difficult to achieve with pale malt, but is not a problem when a significant amount of roast malt is present in the grist because of the higher acidity of dark malts. Therefore, it is difficult to brew a good pale ale or lager from high carbonate water, whereas it would be ideal for producing a stout or porter. So, pale ales were best produced in areas where the water contained much sulphate, such as Burton, and the best porters and stouts came from London and Dublin.

I think it is easy to get too involved in this question of water character. It is extremely difficult to match the chemical constituents of one natural water with another simply by adding various salts. In chemical terms you are trying to change the concentration of individual ions, but salts, by definition, are a mixture of at least two ions, so while you may be changing one, you must also change another. To allow for that, you may have to add another salt, which may change the concentration of yet a third ion, and so on.

While there may be some advantage in adding certain salts, I think it is better to look at the matter another way. First of all, modern malting technology has lead to products which are much more able to cope with slight variations in water quality than was the case a hundred or more years ago. Secondly, since we now know that it is the *pH of the mash* that is important, it is better to concentrate on adjusting that, rather than matching the analysis of a particular water supply.

Nevertheless, since London water was particularly suited to the production of porter, perhaps there is something to learn by looking at its constituents. During the last century it came from deep wells in London, a city surrounded by the vast chalk deposits that make up much of southeastern England - that is what makes the White Cliffs of Dover white! Chalk is, of course, calcium carbonate, so that London well water is high in carbonates. Which I think is the reason why that water happens to be ideal for making tea, but that's another story.

Analysis of water gives only concentrations of individual ions and cannot give the concentrations of minerals which originally dissolved by the water. For convenience, I shall simply use parts per million (milligrams per liter), rather than the more complicated units often used by the water treating industry. So here is a list of the concentrations of the more important ions in London well water:

ION	CONCENTRATION, ppm
Calcium	50
Magnesium	20
Sodium	100
Carbonate	160
Sulfate	80
Chloride	60

Note that this analysis includes only the major ionic species, and that for convenience I have rounded off the figures so that they may not balance exactly in terms of chemical equivalents.

There is an apparent contradiction here for those of you who have read *Pale Ale*, for this shows London water containing less carbonate than Burton water! The explanation is simply that the latter also contains considerably higher levels of calcium, magnesium and sulfate, enough to overcome the effects of the carbonate and make it suitable for pale ale brewing. London water, on the other hand, has a much lower total ionic concentration that is dominated by the carbonate ion.

The high carbonate level in this water makes it alkaline, so that it tends to drive up mash pH if only a pale malt is used. There are just not enough calcium and sulfate ions to keep down the pH, since these ions are less effective at pushing it down than carbonate is at pushing it up. If some dark, roasted malt is added to the grist, it has enough acidity of its own to counteract the effect of carbonate and keep the mash pH within the desired range.

The effect of the various ions on beer flavor is also important. Sulphate ions tend to give the beer a rather dry character and enhance hop bitterness, so the relatively low levels of this ion in London water help to keep hop bitterness from dominating the beer's palate. This water also contains relatively high levels of sodium and chloride ions, which have little effect on mashing, but do influence taste, generally giving the beer a more rounded and fuller flavor. Both of these effects are obviously desirable in brewing a balanced, smooth beer such as porter.

Because of the wide variation in water quality throughout the United States, it is impossible to tell you exactly how to treat your own supply in order to match London water. The first step to take is to obtain an analysis, so that you know exactly what you have. If you are on a public supply, the utility will supply this free. Depending upon the area, and exactly where the company sources its water, there may be considerable variation in water quality throughout the year. It is therefore worth requesting several analyses, or at least getting an analysis performed during the period when you are brewing.

If you have your own well, you may have to pay for an analysis at a local laboratory; this may cost $20 to $30, but you generally only have to do it once, since such supplies usually have a fairly constant composition. Another approach is to contact a supplier of water softening equipment, since they will often perform a water analysis either free or for a nominal sum.

If the water looks clear and tastes and smells good, then all you have to worry about is its ionic content. If it smells unpleasant, tastes brackish or sulfury, contains suspended solids, is colored, or the analysis shows high levels of organic materials or excessive amounts of iron, some treatment is necessary. This can involve carbon filtration and/or ion exchange treatment, which can be expensive, but in such cases you will probably need to clean it up for drinking as well as for brewing. If you have water like this, consult a water treatment professional or find another source for brewing purposes!

Drinking water is classified into three fairly broad categories: soft (less than 100 ppm total dissolved solids), medium hard (100 to 400 ppm t.d.s.), and very hard (400 to 600 ppm t.d.s.). Soft water lends itself most readily to manipulation and can fairly easily be adjusted to make it suitable for brewing a wide variety of beers. In fact, the analysis I gave you for London water puts it in the bottom range for very hard water.

It is important to understand that there are two types of hardness, permanent and temporary. The latter refers to hardness which is removed on boiling and is caused by the presence of carbonate. Permanent hardness, as you might expect from the name, is not removed by boiling and is due to the presence of calcium and magnesium ions. For porter, we are looking mainly for temporary hardness. High levels of permanent hardness are generally associated with high levels of sulfate, which result in a harsher hop bitterness than this style of beer requires.

So what should we look for our water for brewing porter? I would suggest you aim at the following target analysis:

ION	CONCENTRATION, ppm.
Calcium	30 to 60
Magnesium	10 to 20
Sodium	60 to 120
Bicarbonate	100 to 150
Chloride	40 to 90
Sulfate	50 to 100
t.d.s.	300 to 450

Before we get into the business of how you might adjust your own supply to meet this target, there are two points I should make. The first is that it may not be necessary to do this if you are brewing from malt extract, since the mashing stage has already been completed by the manufacturer. However, you might find it worthwhile to add some chloride (as sodium chloride) to soften the beer's flavor. This can be particularly important if your water is high in permanent hardness, which is difficult to reduce and can, as we have seen, put the beer out of balance.

The second point, on which I must finally come clean, is that carbonate is generally present as the bicarbonate ion. That, and not carbonate, is what you will get in your analysis, which is why I have used bicarbonate in the target analysis above. The fact that I have talked only about carbonate up to now may be a little confusing. This arises because carbonate and bicarbonate actually exist together in chemical equilibrium in water, and the point of equilibrium depends upon how much carbon dioxide is dissolved in the water. For our purposes, we can take the

Porter

simple approach that the terms carbonate and bicarbonate are equivalent.

Despite its importance, I am going to leave adjustment of carbonate levels until last. Calcium, magnesium and sulfate levels can be raised by addition of gypsum and Epsom salts. Gypsum is calcium sulfate ($CaSO_4.2H_2O$), and one gram in five gallons of water will add 12 ppm calcium and 30 ppm sulfate. Epsom salts are magnesium sulphate ($MgSO_4.7H_2O$), and one gram in five gallons of water will add five ppm magnesium and 21 ppm sulfate. Since calcium, for a variety of reasons, is the more important ion, concentrate on adjusting this and keep additions of Epsom salts down to avoid making sulfate levels too high. If that means magnesium levels are lower than I suggested in the target analysis, do not worry; that is less important than ensuring that you do not have too much sulfate.

Adjusting sodium and chloride levels is done by addition of sodium chloride (NaCl) or common salt (make sure it is not the iodized type, as this will severely inhibit yeast performance). In this case, one gram of salt in five gallons will add 21 ppm sodium and 32 ppm chloride. Of these, chloride is the more beneficial, so put in enough salt to reach the target level of this ion and do not be concerned if this puts sodium over the top.

Now back to carbonate, which is the most difficult ion to adjust. The first problem is that carbonate-carbon dioxide-bicarbonate equilibrium I referred to. If you adjust the carbonate content of cold water and then boil it (as you should do if you have a highly chlorinated water, as is often the case if it is a public supply), then you drive off the dissolved carbon dioxide. That pushes the equilibrium firmly in favor of the carbonate ion. In the presence of calcium insoluble calcium carbonate precipitates, and your level of dissolved carbonate drops substantially.

78

Label courtesy of American Breweriana Association.

The other problem is that most of the homebrewing literature suggests that you increase carbonate content by adding the requisite amount of precipitated chalk. That makes sense, doesn't it, for London water picked up its carbonate from chalk, didn't it? I am afraid it just is not that simple. Calcium carbonate is really not very soluble in water. In the absence of carbon dioxide, the maximum you can get into solution is five ppm calcium, and seven ppm carbonate!

A better approach would be to add the required amount of precipitated chalk directly to the mash, stirring well, or even to use a soluble salt, such as sodium carbonate. If you use the latter, make sure it is a food grade, such as baking soda, which is actually sodium bicarbonate ($NaHCO_3$). One gram of this in five gallons of water will add 38 ppm bicarbonate *and* 15 ppm sodium.

Frankly, I think it is best not to worry about adjusting carbonate at all! It does not affect flavor, for the simple reason that after the wort boil, there will not be any carbonate left, so it will not reach the finished beer. Take the water you have and check mash acidity; if it is pH 5.0 to 5.5, you need do nothing more. If it is higher than that, the most likely reason will be *too much* carbonate rather than too little, and you need to reduce it by boiling the water before mashing.

EQUIPMENT

I shall not spend much time on this, for porter really requires no special equipment, and I assume that you are already a brewer and have the basic equipment. Malt extract brewers need a boiling pot, preferably of stainless steel, with a large enough capacity to boil the whole brew length. If you have a smaller pot, there is no problem except that your wort is at higher than original gravity during the boil. That will tend to reduce your hop utilization, so you might have to hop at a slightly higher rate than indicated in the recipes in order to attain the same level of bitterness.

If you are stove mashing, you clearly need a pot big enough to handle the mash and to double as the boiler. You will also need some form of lauter tun, to separate the wort from the grain. These are well-described in the homebrewing literature. If you use the picnic cooler system for mashing, runoff can be directly from the cooler, and there is no need for a separate lauter tun. Nowadays you do not even have to make your own mashing system, as several complete mashing setups, one or two of them even with computerized control, are on the market. Any of these are fine for porter.

I do recommend that you employ some form of rapid cooling after boiling, so as to ensure a good cold break and to reduce the risk of infection of the wort. I prefer a simple copper coil, connected to the cold water supply, which is just dropped into the boiler. Systems where the wort flows through a copper coil surrounded by a tube through which water flows in the opposite direction to the wort can be either fabricated or purchased. These work very well but are more difficult to clean than an immersion cooling coil.

A primary fermenter is, of course, essential. This can be an open or closed plastic vessel, although the former can be risky to use, unless you employ a true top-fermenting yeast, which forms a "skin" on top of the beer. An oversized (a capacity of about one gallon more than the brew length) glass carboy is excellent, or you can use a smaller carboy and the blowoff technique. Personally, I do not like the latter; it results in the loss of both beer and some of the hop bittering principles you worked so hard to put into the brew in the first place. It can also be dangerous if you add leaf hops during the fermentation, since the hops can block the tube, and the pressure from the evolved carbon dioxide could cause an explosion.

Though not strictly necessary, a secondary fermenter is very useful for porter. As we have seen, it is a beer that requires maturation, especially if you want to brew at the higher end of the style's gravity range. Maturation can be done in bottle or in the keg from which the beer will be served, but it is arguably better done in bulk. If you want to take this path, I strongly recommend that you use *only* a glass fermenter, filled close to the top, and fitted with a fermentation lock. Long-term storage of any beer in plastic vessels should be avoided, because the plastic is permeable to air.

Porter is a beer which is well-suited to bottling if that is how you wish to handle it. If you prefer to use a keg, that is fine too. The various plastic vessels on the market work reasonably well, although you must be careful that you do not lose carbon dioxide pressure in these if the beer is stored for long periods. In this respect, the stainless steel soda keg systems which are now widely available are excellent, although somewhat expensive.

You could also cask your porter in the traditional

British manner. That was, after all, how it was originally served. Be careful though, for a small wooden cask (that is six to twelve gallons) has a large surface area to volume ratio, so that the beer's conditioning is easily lost through the porous staves. That does not matter if the beer is only in cask long enough to condition, but it can be a serious problem if it is matured in the cask for several months or more.

The technique for using wooden casks I have described elsewhere (*Pale Ale, Classic Beer Style Series*, pp. 67 to 84, Brewers Publications, 1990). It requires a lot of work, but if you are prepared to do it, the feeling of satisfaction in brewing an authentic "real ale" and maintaining a centuries-old tradition is well worthwhile.

As far as microbrewers are concerned, there is little to say about equipment. Porter is a very straightforward, infusion-mashed, top-fermented beer. If you have built a microbrewery without any mash-tun, brewkettle, whirlpool, heat exchanger and fermenter you are beyond help from me! These are pretty much standard, readily available equipment that you should already have. You may, especially if you are bottling the brew, want to have a filter. Also, bear in mind that if you want to make a high-gravity, long-matured porter, you have to have sufficient vessel capacity to handle that and still be able to produce your normal brews!

4

Porter Brewing Procedures

EXTRACT BREWING

There is no special approach involved here. Adjust the ionic content of the water, if desired, and dissolve up the extract. Crush or grind the crystal and roast malts (see under grain mashing) and mix with three to four pints of water. Bring to a boil, strain out the grains, add the liquor to the extract solution, and then proceed with the boil. You can, if you prefer, add the grains to the boil, but you may extract some husk flavor if you do so, and this will stick out like a sore thumb in the flavor of the finished beer.

If you wish to use the partial mash approach to give the beer a little extra body, you can include the roast malts at this point, rather than extracting their flavor separately. For an average porter, you will need to mash around two pounds of pale malt. Grind this carefully, along with the crystal and roast malts, and add to two to three quarts (1.9 to 2.8L) at 161 to 165 degrees F (71.5 to 74 degrees C). Stir well and the mash should settle out to around 154 to 157 degrees F (68 to 69.5 degrees C). This is a fairly high mash temperature, which will give a relatively high proportion of body-building dextrins, which is what we are after, rather than producing fermentable extract.

Hold the mash as close as you can to 154 to 157 degrees F (68 to 69.5 degrees C) for 45 minutes to one hour. It is important to stir vigorously whenever heat is applied, to ensure that it is evenly distributed throughout the bulk of the mash. At completion take the temperature up to around 170 degrees F (77 degrees C), and strain off the liquid into your boiling pot. Rinse the residual grains with two to three quarts (1.9 to 2.8L) of hot water at around 170 degrees F (77 degrees C) and add this to the boiler. Dissolve up the extract, add the remaining water, and you are ready for the boil.

GRAIN MASHING

Grinding of the malt is the first step, and it is something which homebrewers rarely do efficiently. What you are aiming to do is to liberate the starch of the grain, so that it is all readily available for dissolution and degradation by the malt enzymes. You will want to keep enough of the grain intact so that it forms a firm, porous filter bed to permit ready runoff of the wort. With highly-modified, two-row malts this requires, in theory, nothing more than cracking the grain, letting out the starchy endosperm, and leaving the husks intact.

In practice, this is not quite so simple, unless you are lucky enough to own or have access to a roller mill. The hand-cranked grain mills used by most homebrewers inevitably leave some of the endosperm unexposed, so that it is impossible to obtain the same level of extract as commercial brewers can achieve with their multi-roller mills. Do not let this push you into going for finer and finer grinding; all that is likely to do is to block up the grain bed so that wort runoff is very slow, or even stops entirely!

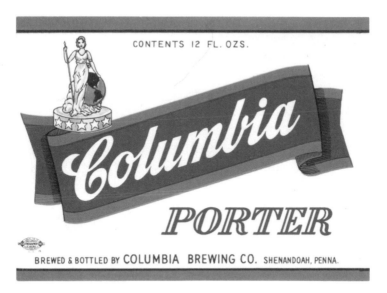

CONTENTS 12 FL. OZS.

Columbia

PORTER

BREWED & BOTTLED BY COLUMBIA BREWING CO. SHENANDOAH, PENNA.

Label courtesy of American Breweriana Association.

It is not essential for the homebrewer to maximize extract yield. Commercial brewers consider it important to do so, but this is for financial, rather than brewing reasons. To the homebrewer, cost is only a part of the picture, and in any case the loss of a little extract represents only a small fraction of the total cost. It is more important to attain *consistent* yields, so that you can calculate approximately how much malt you need to reach a required original gravity. An extract yield of 25 to 30 °/pound/gallon (one pound of malt gives one gallon of wort at OG 1.025 to 1.030 (6.2 to 7.5 °Plato) is perfectly acceptable for brewing quality beer.

It is not actually necessary to do your own grinding, since several suppliers offer preground malt. The extra cost is small, and the product usually gives good extract yield. The disadvantage of doing it this way is that you should only buy in small quantities. It is difficult to store ground malt for any length of time, as it picks up moisture very easily. When this happens, the malt becomes what is known as "slack," and extract yields drop sharply.

Crystal and roast malts are included along with the pale malt in grinding. These are generally more friable than pale malt, and it is their flavors, rather than extracts, we want, so it is not so critical as to how they are ground. Whatever setting works for the pale malt will comfortably handle the specialty malts. Of course, the extract brewer will need to grind these separately. This is no big deal, for it can easily be carried out in a small coffee grinder, or even in a kitchen blender, since only relatively small amounts are involved.

Microbrewers will obviously have a different approach and be aiming for as high an extract yield as possible. You should have a suitable roller mill; ideally, this should be of the two-stage variety. A single-stage mill will work fairly well with highly-modified two-row pale malts, but the double-stage type is more efficient in the long term. If you decide to use the less-modified six-row malts, a somewhat finer grind is needed to ensure maximum extract recovery, and it is essential to use a two- or even three-stage mill.

Mashing in porter brewing is straightforward. If you use British pale malt, a one-step infusion mash at around 150 degrees F (65.5 degrees C) is all that you need. The exact mashing temperature can vary a little, according to the target original gravity of the wort. If you are aiming at below OG 1.050 (12.3 °Plato), you may want to push the infusion temperature up to around 153 degrees F (67 degrees C), to increase the proportion of dextrins in the wort and give the beer a little more body. Do not overdo this, as most of the body and mouthfeel of this type of beer comes from the crystal and roast malts. Since porter should be well-attenuated and have a good alcohol content, too high a level of dextrins will tend to unbalance the beer.

If you are using a U.S. two- or six-row malt you should consider a so-called protein rest, at 120 to 125 degrees F (49 to 51.5 degrees C), before going up to the saccharification step at around 153 degrees F (67 degrees C). Homebrewers who find it a problem to incorporate such a step should not worry. Most modern U.S. malts are sufficiently well-modified that they can be mashed by single-step infusion. However, a protein rest with such malts is good brewing practice and helps to avoid later problems, such as chill haze formation in the beer. I also find that this step helps to improve extract yields a little, and I recommend that you do use it if at all possible.

You need to use one quart of water (0.95L) per pound of malt. Add any required water treatment and heat to 158 to 161 degrees F (70 to 71.5 degrees C); if you use a picnic cooler mash-tun, you will have to have the water 5 to 10 degrees F (3 to 6 degrees C) hotter, since there will be a drop in temperature when it is transferred to the mash-tun. Once you are at the strike temperature add the grains, stirring in well and breaking up any lumps. The mash temperature should settle out to the required 150 to 153 degrees F (65.5 to 67 degrees C). Keep it there for 1 1/2 hours, check for starch conversion with iodine, raise the temperature to about 170 degrees F (76.5 degrees C), and start wort runoff.

Sparge the grains with water (suitably treated, as for mashing) at 170 to 175 degrees F (76.5 to 79.5 degrees C), keeping the level of liquid just above the bed, so that it does not dry out and cause channeling. For a five gallon brew length, you need enough sparge water to give a maximum of six gallons of wort. The actual amount of wort you should collect will depend upon how much is lost in boiling. Commercial brewers conduct sparging quite slowly, taking several hours to complete it in some cases. Most homebrewers find this impractical and use much shorter sparge times, which is one reason why they get lower extract yields than do the professionals.

In any case, sparging is not something that should be overdone, just to push up yield a little. Towards the end of sparging, the pH of the mash tends to rise, and silcates, tannins and polyphenols can be extracted from the grain. These can result in hazes and harsh off-flavors in the finished beer. To avoid this kind of problem, it is probably good practice to stop collecting wort once the gravity of the runoff has fallen to around 1.008 to 1.010 (2.0 to 2.5 °Plato).

WORT BOILING

This is a very important part of the brewing process. Inadequate or careless boiling can result in beer haze problems, failure to reach the required level of hop bitterness, and even loss of valuable wort! The process is the same, whether you brew from extract or grain, except that many extract brewers use only a partial brew length in the boil. Several things happen during boiling:

- The hop alpha acids are extracted, and converted to iso-alpha-acids

- Hop character and aroma are extracted, if aroma hops are used

- Through the formation of the hot break and later the cold break, subsequent haze-forming reactions in the beer are largely eliminated

- Infecting organisms which may be present in the wort are destroyed

- Some caramelization and coloring of the wort occurs

- Evaporation of excess liquor reduces wort volume to the desired brew length

Perhaps the most important of these is the extraction of hop bitterness. There are two phases to this, the first being extraction of alpha acids from the hops, and the second is their chemical conversion to iso-alpha-acids, which are the real source of hop bitterness in beer. The problem is that alpha acids are not very soluble in wort, and that the conversion to iso-alpha-acid is relatively slow at the pH of wort. The solution is to ensure that you have a vigorous, so-called "rolling boil" so that the resin droplets are continually being broken up and thoroughly mixed with the hot wort. Then maximum conversion to iso-alpha-acids will occur only if sufficient boiling time is allowed, usually one to one-and-a-half hours.

A vigorous boil also helps the formation of the hot break, that is coagulation of the higher molecular weight protein residues. These are capable of complexing with tannins from the malt and hops, and the complexes will precipitate and cause hazes when the beer is cooled. It is therefore important for beer stability to remove them as completely as possible at this stage. Note that hot break formation is usually favored by the presence of calcium ions. Malt extract brewers who have *not* treated a soft water supply might find it advantageous to add one to two grams of gypsum at the start of the boil.

Bittering hops should be added at the start of the boil, or as some brewers prefer, after the first 10 to 15 minutes, when the white flakes of the hot break first become visible. If you are adding aroma hops, these can be added at intermediate stages, usually during the last 20 minutes of boiling, or even after the heating has been turned off. It is impossible to make precise recommendations here, except to point out that the essential oils of hops, which yield hop aroma, are volatile and will be driven off from the wort during boiling. Therefore, you will get different results with the same aroma hop, depending upon when you add it.

My own preference is to add the stronger-flavored hops, such as Northern Brewer and Eroica, 15 to 20 minutes before the end. Very fragrant varieties, like Cascade, Hallertauer and Talisman seem best when added five to fifteen minutes before completion. On the other hand, the traditional English Goldings, Styrian Goldings and Saaz are more effective when added *after* the heat is turned off.

Caramelization is not something you should worry about too much. There will always be some darkening of the wort during boiling, but this is not a problem with a beer like porter, and a little extra caramel will only add to its flavor. It is possible to mar the beer's flavor if you have a hot spot in the boiler, and some charring of the malt sugars should occur. This is not likely to be the case if you are using a stainless steel pot, but it is something to watch for if you have an electric boiler, especially one where the element is outside the boiler and not in the wort. It is a risk when you scale up to larger volumes if the heat source is a very hot one applied to only a small part of the bottom surface of the kettle. The remedy is simply to spread out the heat, either by means of a ring burner, or by using more than one source.

Evaporation and concentration of the wort will always occur and is of course desirable for the mashing brewer, who will have started with rather more than the final brew length. Commercial brewers usually achieve around 10 percent evaporation during boiling, but homebrewers will usually lose quite a bit more with a proper vigorous boil, because they are working with a much higher surface area to volume ratio. There is no need to be concerned about this. All you need to do after cooling is to top up to brew length with sterile water.

As to cooling, I just want to emphasize that, as I discussed under equipment, it is essential to cool the boiled wort as rapidly as possible. This is important from the point of view of avoiding infection and for bringing about good cold break formation. The latter is mainly low molecular weight protein degradation products, which do not coagulate very well with slow cooling and are thus difficult to remove. And if they are not removed, they can both inhibit yeast 'growth' and form very persistent chill hazes in the finished beer.

Rapid and complete cooling down to fermentation temperatures will help these materials to coagulate well enough so that they can be removed with the rest of the trub. Some kind of cooling coil (or heat exchanger for microbrewers) is essential. This might seem like an extra complication, but it can really be done very simply, and it will help you to finish your brewing day quicker and give you more time to sample the results!

Finally, always take care to remove the trub as completely as possible, since it can inhibit yeast growth. Microbrewers will probably find a whirlpool the best way to go, while the homebrewer will have to rely on siphoning. I think it best to look at cooling and trub removal this way: the cleaner the wort is when it is pitched with yeast, then the cleaner will be the flavor of the finished beer.

FERMENTATION

We have already seen that some porters are produced with bottom-fermenting yeasts. You can do that too, if you like, but I think the estery notes from a top-fermenting or ale

Inside Boulder Brewing Co., Boulder, Colo.

yeast are more suited to this style of beer. I am therefore going to limit my comments to the use of ale yeasts.

The most important consideration in the primary fermentation is that of temperature, with 60 to 68 degrees F (15.5 to 20 degrees C) being the optimum range. Lower temperatures are not advisable, as the yeast may struggle, and it may not be possible to reach the desired level of attenuation. Temperatures a few degrees above the top end of this range are acceptable, but if you cannot get below 75 degrees F (24 degrees C), you have a real problem.

High fermentation temperatures result in excessive production of higher alcohols (fusel oils), esters and diacetyl, and may also result in a significant loss of iso-alpha-acids (and therefore bitterness). Too much fusel oil will give the beer a harsh taste, and a high level of esters will result in a loss of balance. Diacetyl, with its typical butterscotch flavor, can be acceptable, but only in very small amounts. You are better off without it, since it can play a part in staling reactions with a beer that is likely to be matured for long periods.

Microbrewers should, in any case, have installed temperature-controlled fermenters, since the heat produced during fermentation is not easily dissipated from a large bulk. For the homebrewer in the United States, the problem is somewhat harder to solve, depending upon ambient temperatures where you live. Of course, a cool constant-temperature basement or cellar is the ideal answer, but is not something you can easily go out and buy if you do not already have one!

As I discussed in *Pale Ale*, temperature control during fermentation has been something with which the homebrewer has had great difficulty. Most people have come up with their own answers, such as "hot boxes" heated by a low-wattage bulb in cold areas, or immersing the carboy in a bath of cold water (which requires frequent changing) in warm areas. A relatively simple approach (providing that you have a separate brewing refrigerator) has become available in the last couple of years. For $50 or so, you can now buy a controller which easily attaches to the refrigerator and will maintain temperatures in our required range, irrespective of outside levels.

With a good active yeast, primary fermentation should be completed in around seven days. By completed, I mean that wort specific gravity will have fallen to close to one-quarter of the original gravity. Fermentation should have slowed right down, with the yeast forming a good compact cake on the bottom of the vessel and a skin on the surface of the beer. If so, it is ready for the next stage.

SECONDARY FERMENTATION AND CELLARING

Providing you have reached the prescribed level of finishing gravity in the primary stage, there is no reason why you could not bottle, keg or cask the beer at this point. However, this is a beer which will definitely improve with keeping and will benefit from a period of secondary fermentation, especially if you are brewing at the higher end of the recommended gravity range.

The duration of secondary fermentation is a debatable question. As we have seen, the original versions may have been stored for as long as a year before being casked and shipped to the customer. I do not really recommend that you should keep your porter in its secondary fermenter for as long as that, or for even a matter of months! Microbrewers will want to avoid it for financial reasons, and homebrewers should avoid it because they will not be able to keep out air for such long periods.

I think microbrewers will find two to three weeks in the secondary, at temperatures 10 to 15 degrees F (5 to 8 degrees C) lower than those for the primary stage, should be sufficient to control yeast levels and to remove unwanted volatiles, such as diacetyl. The beer's flavor may still be a little unbalanced at this point, but it will continue to mature and improve in either bottle or keg.

Homebrewers should rack the beer into a glass carboy taking care not to splash it, so as to minimize oxygen pickup. The carboy must be filled right up to the neck and fitted with an airlock. It can be left here several weeks *if* it is still fermenting slowly, so that the vessel continues to hold a slight positive carbon dioxide pressure. Once this disappears, *even with an airlock*, air will eventually diffuse back through the lock into the beer. And when that happens, oxidation and staling reactions will take place, and your prized brew will develop all sorts of off-flavors.

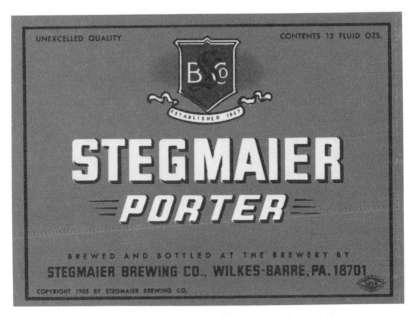

Label courtesy of American Breweriana Association.

You must therefore carefully monitor the carboy, and as soon as gas ceases to be evolved from the beer, it must be racked into a sealed container (keg or bottle). This may take several weeks, for yeasts often slowly break down the lower dextrins into fermentable sugars. If it takes only one to two weeks to stop fermenting entirely, do not worry that it might not yet be fully matured. It is better to rack it immediately and let it mature in bottle or keg before drinking, rather than risk letting air get in to spoil the beer.

Basically, secondary fermentation is best carried out at 50 to 55 degrees F (10 to 13 degrees C), which is quite typical for an English cellar. Higher temperatures will result in a quicker end to fermentation, and probably a quicker flavor maturation, but should not otherwise harm the beer. This is a good time to dry-hop the beer, should you wish to do so. It is a technique widely practiced by British pale ale and bitter brewers and lends the beer a unique hop aroma, though it might be a little overpowering in a porter.

Use no more than one-half ounce hops per five gallons. Leaf hops are better than pellets for this purpose, in terms of aroma, but can cause problems of siphon hose blocking when it comes to racking. Also, if you are putting the beer into a soda keg, any hop leaves that get into the keg can easily block the outlet lines. In such a case, it is probably safer to dry hop with pellets. You can naturally use any hop variety you like, but I prefer the traditional Goldings. Be careful though; dry-hopping puts a lot of hop oil into the beer, and this can easily oxidize and cause it to have an unpleasant rancid flavor. Do not do it unless you are very careful to keep out air and can keep the secondary fermentation below 65 degrees F (18 degrees C).

PACKAGING

I should have made it plain by now that there are few hard and fast rules about porter. Originally it may have been a "real ale," served only on draught; you can still handle it that way, or you can bottle it. Indeed, porter makes an excellent naturally-conditioned bottled beer, whose flavor will tend to mellow with aging.

Should you prefer to filter and artificially carbonate it, you can do so. Filtration systems are now readily available to the amateur as well as to the microbrewer. Properly handled they will give a clear, colloidally stable beer with low oxygen levels. Filtration certainly does remove something from the beer, for it takes out some of the larger proteinaceous molecules which affect both mouthfeel and head retention. It can be argued that a high-gravity, all-malt porter has plenty of these characteristics to spare, so that the loss of a small portion will not be noticed.

I would argue that a beer which needs to have all its flavor components balanced will be at its best when naturally conditioned. I am not able to prove it scientifically, but it does seem that beers of this type mature better in the presence of yeast. Filtering (especially if followed by pasteurization) seems to "freeze" the beer flavor, so that little subsequent change occurs.

There may be market reasons which force a microbrewer to filter, but I cannot recommend it to the homebrewer. Careful brewing and pouring technique should ensure that the beer will be clear. In any case, its color is dark enough that it does not need the brilliant clarity of a pale beer. Further, the presence of yeast helps to reduce the dangers of off-flavor formation through oxidation by dissolved air.

Microbrewers may consider pasteurization necessary, since they have no control over the beer once it leaves the brewery. This process does stabilize a filtered beer but can also give it a cooked flavor, which I find objectionable. A better alternative is that of sterile filtration through a membrane. This first requires a standard diatomaceous earth filtration and then careful handling of the beer after passing through the membrane. As a filtration, it will remove some flavor characteristics of the beer and perhaps limit further flavor modification with aging, but it is usually less damaging than pasteurization.

The final point to consider about packaging porter is carbonation. As I indicated in the profile section, porter is a beer which can stand relatively high levels of carbon dioxide. Let me restate that this should not be overdone, unless you really do prefer soda to beer! Like all the other aspects of porter flavor, carbonation must be part of the balance. The draught real porters now available in England generally contain around one volume of CO_2, while bottled versions there and here in the United States go up as high as 2.5 volumes.

Label courtesy of American Breweriana Association.

I think the last figure is a little high and would prefer not to go above two volumes for bottled porter. And I still like to keep my draught porter at around one volume; the lower gas level really does make for a smoother drink. Of course, in quoting these figures, I am assuming a serving temperature of about 50 to 55 degrees F (10 to 13 degrees C). Volume levels decrease as the temperature is lowered and increase when it goes up for the same level of carbonation.

After secondary fermentation, the beer is going to contain around 0.4 to 0.5 volumes CO_2. Therefore, if you add two ounces cane sugar, or 2 1/2 ounces corn sugar per five gallons you will increase by 0.8 volumes, giving a final figure of around 1.2 volumes. This is just right for the draught beer, so this is the level of priming you need for kegging or casking.

With the plastic style keg, or the stainless steel soda kegs, this priming will probably be insufficient to dispense all the beer. In either instance, all you need to do is to wait until flow almost ceases and then add a little more carbon dioxide, either from a bulb in the case of the plastic vessels, or from your cylinder in the case of the soda keg. With the latter, I recommend that you set your control gauge at five psi as a maximum, and that the gas is only left on while the beer is actually being served.

The stainless steel keg approach enables you to avoid priming entirely, since the beer can be carbonated directly from the cylinder. It might appear that all you need to do is to turn on the gas supply, set the gauge at 4 to 5 psi, and leave it that way until you are ready to drink the beer. Surprisingly, this approach does not work very well, unless the gas is left on for a matter of weeks. This method is more effective if the beer has been well-cooled, the gauge set at 20 psi, and the keg is vigorously shaken at intervals.

It is easy to overdo carbonation by this approach. Knowing my aversion to high carbon dioxide levels, you will not be surprised to learn that I do not advocate it! In the long run priming as described above, supplying only enough gas from the cylinder as is needed for dispense, is just as simple and more reliable.

In the case of bottled porter, priming the beer with 3 1/2 ounces of cane sugar or 4 1/4 ounces corn sugar in five gallons will increase the carbonation level by around 1.4 volumes. That will give a final level of about 1.9 volumes, which is just right. I know that American taste is towards much higher levels of carbonation, but why go to such lengths to put all that flavor in your beer, then smother it with mere gas?

SERVING

I think the primary point here is the temperature of the beer. As a fairly robust style, porter can still be quite tasty at temperatures close to freezing. However, much of its character and nuance will be lost if it is drunk really cold. Tradition says it should be drunk at cellar temperature or 50 to 55 degrees F (10 to 13 degrees C), which is cool and not warm. I think there is more to it than just tradition, for this is just about the right range to bring out all the aspects of the flavor of this complex beer. Colder temperatures tend to inhibit mouthfeel and body characteristics. The roasted malt flavors can be over-emphasized, making the black malt taste stand out and ruin the beer's balance.

People in the United States just do not have a proper reverence for beer. I think this is most obviously demonstrated by the widespread habit of drinking straight from the bottle or can. If you really respect the brewer's efforts (which may be your own), you should always use a glass to show the beer off to best advantage. How else can you properly admire a well-formed head, inhale the enticing aroma, or be enticed by a seductive, warming color?

No winemaker worth the name would serve his product from a colored tumbler, and you too should select your porter glass with care. It is *not* just "suds"; it is a complex, intriguing and stylish brew and should be served accordingly! I like the thin pint glass known as a "sleeve" for a lower gravity porter, and the stemmed tulip shape half-pint glass for stronger porter. The glass mug (sometimes mistakenly called a tankard) is available in many styles. Although it is often an attractive drinking vessel, it does tend to hide the rich warm colors of porter. The choice is up to you, but I am convinced that if the brewer thinks enough of his beer to serve it in an attractive glass, he will surely have put in the effort to have made the beer worth drinking!

5

Porter Recipes

I am going to describe several recipes for various styles of porter. Each one will include details for a five gallon (18.9L) malt extract brew, a five gallon (18.9L) grain mash, and for the microbrewer a one barrel (1.17 hL) grain mash. This does not mean that these three brews would be identical, but they should be quite similar in flavor.

In order to keep things from becoming too complicated, I have had to make some assumptions and take some short cuts. For example, I have included metric units only as a direct conversion from U.S. units. If you prefer the metric system, you will probably want to work at a more convenient brewlength, such as 20L, rather than 18.9L. If you do that, then *all* ingredient levels must be adjusted by the same factor in order to achieve a similar result.

Because of the difficulties discussed in the section on ingredients, no further comments are made on water treatment. It is assumed you have followed those recommendations or decided to simply go with whatever water you have. Just remember that if you do not treat the water and are unsatisfied with the beer's flavor, this could be just as much of the problem as any other part of the brewing process.

For the mash brews I have assumed that you will be using British two-row pale malt, but you can of course substitute that with U.S. two- or even six-row pale malt. Original gravities are given on the basis of extract yields for pale malt of 30 °/pound/gallon for the homebrewer and 35 °/pound/gallon for the microbrewer. If you cannot achieve these numbers in your own setup, do not worry, just adjust the amount of malt to allow for whatever extract yield you do obtain. Crystal, chocolate and black malts, as well as roasted barley, have all been assumed to give 25 °/pound/ gallon, which should be close enough in most cases. I assume that you will be using the more highly-roasted, highest-colored (about 90 to 100 °L) crystal malts.

In the case of the malt extract brew, it is assumed that these specialty malts have been mixed with water, taken just to the boil, then strained off, and the liquor added to the brew. Malt extract syrups have been taken as giving 36 °/pound/gallon while powdered extract is put at 45 °/pound/gallon. If pale malt is recommended in an extract recipe, this implies that you will need to treat it by the partial-mash technique described in the section on brewing procedures.

All the recipes are based on a 1 1/2 hour boil, with bittering hops added at the beginning or just after the first signs of hot break formation. In calculating IBUs of each brew, no allowance has been made for any contribution to bittering from aroma hops added at later intervals during the boil. The calculations also assume 25 percent utilization in the five gallon brews and 30 percent for the one barrel brewlength. Microbrewers who have determined exact utilization rates from analysis of their beers should recalculate hopping rates on this basis. Naturally, if you are using hops whose alpha acid analysis differs from that given in each recipe, you will also have to recalculate the amount required to give the recommended level of bittering.

The color levels given must be regarded as being only approximate numbers. The exact color of your brew will depend not only on the color of the malts actually used, but also on the degree of browning occurring during boiling. In the later comments on each of these recipes, I shall remark on the visual appearance of these beers.

I have not made specific recommendations on particular strains of yeast to be used, since too many outside factors dictate this choice. I have, however, assumed that it will be a top-fermenting variety, and that you will follow my earlier prescriptions on fermentation temperatures.

Specific recommendations as to packaging and aging will be made for each brew. You do not have to do it this way; just remember that if you do package differently, you will probably want to adjust priming and therefore the carbonation level. These recommendations, as well as those for hopping rates and the suggested hop varieties, are to be regarded only as guidelines. The recipes given should produce some excellent porters, but represent only a few of the possibilities available to the imaginative brewer. Between original gravities, hop variety and hop rates, levels and types of roast malt, and different strains of yeasts, you have a large number of variables to play with in putting together a porter. If every reader of this book comes up with a unique version of the style, I shall be well-satisfied, especially if I get to taste most of them!

POPULAR PALE PORTER.

Length	5 gallons (Grain)	5 gallons (Extract)	1 barrel (Grain)
Pale malt:	7.5 lb (3.5 kg)	_____	40 lb (18.25 kg)
Crystal malt:	0.5 lb (227 g)	0.5 lb (227 g)	3.2 lb (1.5 kg)
Pale malt syrup:	_____	6 lb (2.7 kg)	_____
Chocolate malt:	4 oz (114 g)	4 oz (114 g)	1.6 lb (0.7 kg)
Bittering hops			
Fuggle (5% alpha):	1.3 oz (37 g)	1.8 oz (37 g)	6.7 oz (190 g)
HBU:	6.5	6.5	33.5
IBU:	24	24	24
Aroma hops			
Goldings (end of boil):	0.5 oz (14 g)	0.5 oz (14 g)	3 oz (85 g)
Color (°L):	35	35	35
Mash temperature:	152 to 153 degrees F (66.5 to 67 degrees C)		
Original Gravity:	1.048 (11.8 °Plato)		
Finishing Gravity:	1.010 to 1.012 (2.5 to 3.0 °Plato)		
Priming sugar:	2 oz (57 g) cane sugar, as syrup, in 5 gallons		
CO_2 (volumes):	1 1/4 to 1 1/2		
Packaging:	Draught		
Maturation time:	One month		

FOSTER'S ENTIRE BUTT

Length	5 gallons (Grain)	5 gallons (Extract)	1 barrel (Grain)
Pale malt:	7.6 lb (3.5 kg)	_____	41 lb (18.6 kg)
Crystal malt:	0.75 lb (340 g)	0.75 lb (340 g)	4.7 lb (2.1 kg)
Pale malt syrup:	_____	6 lb (2.7 kg)	_____
Pale dry extract:	_____	6 oz (170 g)	_____
Chocolate malt:	0.5 lb (227 g)	0.5 lb (227 g)	3.25 lb (1.5 kg)
Bittering hops			
N.Brewer (9% alpha):	1 oz (28 g)	1 oz (28 g)	5.1 oz (145 g)
HBU:	9	9	45.9
IBU:	33	33	33
Aroma hops			
Hallertauer			
(10 minutes):	0.5 oz (14 g)	0.5 oz (14 g)	3 oz (85 g)
Color (°L):	50	50	50

Mash temperature:	151 to 152 degrees F (66 to 66.5 degrees C)
Original Gravity:	1.052 (12.8 °Plato)
Finishing Gravity:	1.011 to 1.013 (2.75 to 3.25 °Plato)
Priming sugar:	3.5 oz (99 g) cane sugar, as syrup, in 5 gallons
CO_2 (volumes):	1.3/4 to 2
Packaging:	In bottle
Maturation time:	One to two months

REDCOAT'S REVENGE PORTER

Length	5 gallons (Grain)	5 gallons (Extract)	1 barrel (Grain)
Pale malt:	8.6 lb (3.9 kg)	1.5 lb (0.7 kg)	46.6 lb (21.2 kg)
Crystal malt:	1 lb (0.45 kg)	1 lb (0.45 kg)	6.3 lb (2.9 kg)
Pale malt syrup:	_____	6 lb (2.7 kg)	_____
Chocolate malt:	0.5 lb (227 g)	0.5 lb (227 g)	3.2 lb (1.5 kg)
Black malt:	2 oz (57 g)	2 oz (57 g)	0.8 lb (0.4 kg)
Bittering hops			
Clusters (7% alpha)	1.7 oz (48 g)	1.7 oz (48 g)	9 oz (256 g)
HBU:	11.9	11.9	63
IBU:	45	45	45
Aroma hops			
Cascade (10 minutes):	0.4 oz (11 g)	0.4 oz (11 g)	2.5 oz (71 g)
Talisman (end):	0.5 oz (14 g)	0.5 oz (14 g)	3 oz (85 g)
Color (°L)	70	70	70

Mash temperature:	150 to 152 degrees F (65.5 to 66.5 degrees C)
Original Gravity:	1.060 (14.7 °Plato)
Finishing Gravity:	1.012 to 1.016 (3.0 to 4.0 °Plato)
Priming sugar:	4 oz (114 g) cane sugar, as syrup, in 5 gallons
CO_2 (volumes):	2 to 2 1/0
Packaging:	In bottle
Maturation time:	2 to 6 months

BOW BELLS BROWN BEER

Length	5 gallons (Grain)	5 gallons (Extract)	1 barrel (Grain)
Pale malt:	6.9 lb (3.1 kg)	_____	37 lb (16.8 kg)
Crystal malt:	0.5 lb (227 g)	0.5 lb (227 g)	3.2 lb (1.5 kg)
Pale malt syrup:	_____	5 lb (2.3 kg)	_____
Pale dry extract:	_____	0.6 lb (272 g)	_____
Chocolate malt:	1 oz (28 g)	1 oz (28 g)	6 oz (170 g)
Black malt:	3 oz (85 g)	3 oz (85 g)	1.2 lb (545 g)
Bittering hops			
Galena (12% alpha)	0.6 oz (17 g)	0.6 oz (17 g)	3.2 oz (91 g)
HBU:	7.2	7.2	38.4
IBU:	27	27	27.5
Aroma hops			
Hallertauer (end):	1 oz (28 g)	1 oz (28 g)	5 oz (142 g)
Color (°L):	35	35	35
Mash temperature:	152 to 154 degrees F (66.5 to 68 degrees C)		
Original Gravity:	1.045 (11.1 °Plato)		
Finishing Gravity:	1.010-1.011 (2.5 to 2.8 °Plato)		
Priming sugar:	2.25 oz (64 g) cane sugar, as syrup, in 5 gallons.		
CO_2 (volumes):	1 1/3		
Packaging:	On draught		
Maturation time:	4 to 6 weeks		

BLACKBEARD'S BUTT BEER

Length:	5 gallons (Grain)	5 gallons (Extract)	1 barrel (Grain)
Pale malt:	7.25 lb (3.3 kg)	_____	39 lb (17.7 kg)
Crystal malt:	0.8 lb (363 g)	0.8 lb (363 g)	5 lb (2.3 kg)
Pale malt syrup:	_____	6 lb (2.7 kg)	_____
Chocolate malt:	4 oz (114 g)	4 oz (114 g)	1.6 lb (0.73 kg)
Black malt:	4 oz (114 g)	4 oz (114 g)	1.6 lb (0.73 kg)
Bittering hops			
Goldings (5% alpha):	1.7 oz (48 g)	1.7 oz (48 g)	9 oz (256 g)
HBU:	8.5	8.5	45
IBU:	32	32	32
Aroma hops			
Tettnanger			
(10 minutes):	0.2oz (7g)	0.2oz (7g)	1oz (28g)
Goldings (end):	0.5 oz (14 g)	0.5 oz (14 g)	3 oz (85 g)
Color (°L):	61	61	61
Mash temperature:	151 to 153 degrees F (66 to 67 degrees C)		
Original Gravity:	1050 (12.3 °Plato)		
Finishing Gravity:	1.011 to 1.013 (2.75 to 3.25 °Plato)		
Priming sugar:	3.5 oz (99 g) cane sugar, as syrup, in 5 gallons.		
CO_2 (volumes):	1 9/10 to 2		
Packaging:	In bottle		
Maturation time:	6 to 10 weeks		

'IGHLY 'OPPED HENTIRE

Length	5 gallons (Grain)	5 gallons (Extract)	1 barrel (Grain)
Pale malt:	7.8lb (3.5Kg)	2lb (0.9Kg)	41.9lb (19.0Kg)
Crystal malt:	1.25 lb (570 g)	1.25 lb (570 g)	7.9 lb (3.6 kg)
Pale malt syrup:	_____	4.8 lb (2.2 kg)	_____
Black malt:	6 oz (170 g)	6 oz (170 g)	2.4 lb (1.1 kg)
Roast barley:	1 oz (28 g)	1 oz (28 g)	6 oz (170 g)
Bittering hops			
Northern Brewer			
(10% alpha):	1.1 oz (31 g)	1.1 oz (31 g)	5.6 oz (159 g)
HBU:	11	11	56
IBU:	41	41	40
Aroma hops			
Northern Brewer			
(20 minutes):	0.2 oz (6 g)	0.2 oz (6 g)	1.25 oz (36 g)
Goldings (end):	1 oz (28 g)	1 oz (28 g)	6 oz (170 g)
Styrian Goldings			
(fermentation dry-hop):		0.5 oz (14 g)	0.5 oz (14 g)
3 oz (85 g)			

Color (°L):	70	70	70
Mash temperature:	151 to 152 degrees F (66 to 66.5 degrees C)		
Original Gravity:	1.055 (13.5 °Plato)		
Finishing Gravity:	1.012 to 1.014 (3.0 to 3.5 °Plato)		
Priming sugar:	2.5 oz (71 g) cane sugar, as syrup, in 5 gallons		
CO_2 (volumes):	1 1/3-1 1/2		
Packaging:	On draught		
Maturation time:	1 to 4 months		

ENTIRELY ENTIRE OR NEW LONDON PORTER

Length	5 gallons (Grain)	5 gallons (Extract)	1 barrel (Grain)
Pale malt:	9.8 lb (4.4 kg)	2 lb (0.9 kg)	52.9 lb (24.0 kg)
Crystal malt:	1.5 lb (680 g)	1.5 lb (680 g)	9.5 lb (4.3 kg)
Pale malt syrup:	_____	6.5 lb (3.0 kg)	_____
Chocolate malt:	0.75 lb (340 g)	0.75 lb (340 g)	4.7 lb (2.1 kg)

Bittering hops

Goldings (5% alpha):	3.25 oz (92 g)	3.25 oz (92 g)	16.8 oz (480 g)
HBU:	16.3	16.3	84
IBU:	61	61	60

Aroma hops

Goldings (end)	1 oz (28 g)	1 oz (28 g)	6 oz (170 g)
Goldings (fermentation dry hop):		0.5 oz (14 g)	0.5 oz (14 g)
3 oz (85 g)			

Color (°L):	85	85	85

Mash temperature: 150 to 152 degrees F (65.5 to 66.5 degrees C)
Original Gravity: 1.070 (17.0 °Plato)
Finishing Gravity: 1.015 to 1.019 (3.8 to 4.8 °Plato)
Priming sugar: 4.5 oz cane sugar, as syrup, in 5 gallons
CO_2 (volumes): 2 1/4 to 2 1/2
Packaging: In bottle
Maturation time: 3 months to ?

NOTES AND COMMENTS ON RECIPE BEERS

Popular Pale Porter. This is a moderate example of the style, relatively low in gravity and hop bitterness. Small proportions of crystal and chocolate malts mean that it is a very red shade, only a little deeper in color than many bitters, which is where the name comes from. The relatively high temperature mash is necessary to give it a little extra body, matched by a light aroma from the mild Fuggle hops. It does not need much maturing and makes an easy-drinking draught beer with little complexity.

Foster's Entire Butt. A very much middle of the road porter of reasonable strength with plenty of crystal and chocolate malt to give a deep red-brown color. The extra chocolate malt roasted flavors are nicely set off by the spiciness of Hallertauer as the aroma hop, and the higher gravity makes it a beer which will improve with limited keeping. You can work out the significance of the name yourself!

Redcoat's Revenge Porter. This is a much stronger beer with a lot of chocolate malt and a little black malt to give a very deep red-black shade. It has to have much more hop bitterness, plus a good deal of hop aroma, to balance the roast malt flavors and high alcohol content. Because of its strength and the many flavor components, it needs a good deal of maturation to achieve a balance, and so is at its best as a bottled beer. I gave it that name on the basis of its using a lot of American hops. If you wanted to make it an even more authentic American porter, you could substitute some of the pale malt with molasses.

Bow Bells Brown Beer. This is the lowest gravity of any of the porters with most of the roast malt character coming from black malt. The touch of chocolate malt ensures it has a red tinge in its black-brown color, and the spiciness of Hallertauer aroma hops nicely offsets the aromatic flavor of the black malt. For this style, it is a relatively simple beer and makes for smooth drinking when served on draught with short maturation times.

Blackbeard's Butt Beer. This gets its name from its higher proportion of black malt. There is also a fair amount of chocolate and plenty of crystal malt, making it a deep black-red color. There is plenty of hop bitterness and aroma, as well as a higher carbonation level to counter balance the roast malts. Although this beer is only of average strength, it will improve markedly on storage and makes a fine bottled beer.

'Ighly 'Opped Hentire. A higher gravity beer with a lot of crystal, just about the maximum amount of black malt, and a touch of roasted barley. That means it needs high hop bitterness and hop aroma from several sources, including fermentation dry hopping with Styrian Goldings. It is a very dark black-brown beer with ample complexity and is excellent on draught with a little higher carbonation than I usually like. This one definitely needs a good maturation period to smooth out all the lumps and corners! The name simply reflects the old Cockney habit of not pronouncing "aitches" at the beginning of a word, except for those words that start with a vowel and have no aitch! Hentire goes down very well with "Kate and Sidney pie"; if you do not know what that is, just think about its Cockney name.

Entirely Entire or New London Porter. Well, I must give you one recipe for a high-gravity original-style porter, mustn't I? Entirely Entire is a very appropriate name, but I gave it a second one for the simple reason that there had to be a reference to Connecticut somewhere in this section! Naturally, this is a strong beer, very high in both chocolate and crystal malt, so that it has a dark deep-red color. All that flavor requires a lot of hop bitterness and a great deal of aroma, which all come from the traditional English Goldings variety. I like to give it a little extra carbonation and bottle it, since it does require long maturation to be at its smooth best. Indeed, it should keep for an indefinite period providing air is carefully excluded during bottling. If you are into strong cheeses, this will sit very nicely with a good ripe Stilton, for it is definitely a beer which should be sipped and savored, rather than just drunk!

6

Commercially Available Porters

In a book of this kind it is important to look at some of the commercial examples of the style, in order to see how they match up with our profile of what the beer should be. Also, they make a good benchmark for anyone wanting to brew the style but is not familiar with it in practice. Perhaps this section should be at the front of the book, since drinking one or two of these examples while reading the text would surely help to illuminate some of my arguments.

Porter is actually not that widely available, partly because it is often regarded as a seasonal style, and partly because it is often a draught-only beer (particularly in England). Also, it is in the main produced by small independents, microbreweries, or brewpubs, so that the selling area of a particular version may be quite limited. A good example of the latter is what appears to be a unique variation of the style: Chinook Alaskan Smoked Porter, apparently sold only in Alaska during the winter.

Therefore, there are a number of porters brewed both in the United States and in England that I have not had the chance to sample. So I am going to keep this list fairly short, restricting it to beers that are either widely distributed or of particular interest. If you want to chase up some more examples read Don Hoag's "The Porters of the United States" (*zymurgy*, Winter 1987, Vol. 10, No. 5, pp. 34 to 38), or James D. Robertson's "American Porter" (*All About Beer*, February 1990, Vol. 11, No. 1, pp. 48 to 49).

AMERICAN PORTERS

Anchor Porter. This has a brown well-formed head and fairly high carbonation. It is very dark, mainly brown-black in color, with the aromatic character of black malt in the nose. The pungent dry taste of black malt is evident in the flavor without overwhelming it, for it is a properly-balanced, smooth-drinking rewarding porter.

Catamount Porter. There is less malt evident in the aroma of this one, which has a red hue to its dark color. It is

Commercially available American porters include Yuengling, Anchor, Sierra Nevada, Catamount and Labatt. Photo by Terry Foster.

not too heavily carbonated, but still forms a good long-lasting head. Nice hop bitterness backs up a not-overdone roasted-coffee flavor of black malt. With good dryness and balance, it would be fantastic with some more hop aroma.

Sierra Nevada Porter. A little over-carbonated to my taste with a big long-lasting, finely-bubbled brownish head. Hops as well as malt come out in the nose, and there is good hop bitterness to back up the black malt burnt flavor. A very complex but still balanced beer, although its color and flavor put it very close to the borderline between robust porter and dry stout. It is definitely a beer worth thinking about!

Yuengling's Pottsville Porter. As I remarked in the text, this is in some senses a classic porter, although it is bottom-fermented. Unfortunately, although it has many adherents, I am not one of them as I find it a little disappointing. It is a very dark black-brown beer with a nicely moderate level of carbonation, but the head collapses quite quickly. Although Pottsville Porter has a fairly smooth, well-balanced flavor without much in the way of roast malt notes or hop bitterness discernible, my overall sensation is that it is far too sweet for the style.

BRITISH PORTERS

Burton Porter. This is notable because it is a bottle-conditioned porter, and because it is brewed by Burton Bridge Brewery in Burton-upon-Trent, the great bastion of pale ale brewing! It has a nice, translucent deep red-brown color with a somewhat yeasty aroma. Unfortunately, in the samples I tasted, there was a very harsh, astringent bitterness which spoiled the beer. It was perhaps an old sample. The

117

British porters available commercially include Original London Porter and Burton Porter. Photo by Terry Foster.

next time I get over to England, I shall try to test it at the source, which might well change my opinion about this beer.

Pimlico Porter. This is significant because it is brewed at the Orange Brewery, a brewpub in Pimlico, London, and is therefore the only remaining example of a London-brewed porter. It is actually an excellent brew, served only on draught. There is a hint of malt in the aroma, it has a nice ruby-red color, good hop bitterness, definite estery character, and all the components blend nicely to give a smooth, very satisfying drink. I recommend you try this beer if you are in the neighborhood, although the pub itself is not the most attractive one I have ever visited!

Pitfield London Porter. As remarked in the text, this is now brewed outside of London to an old Whitbread recipe. A brew with a very aromatic malty aroma and a long-lasting brown head. It is very dark in color, though with definite ruby tints. The typical black malt, dry roasted coffee flavor comes through nicely and is very well-balanced by the hop bitterness and alcohol content. It really is a first-rate example of the style when properly matured.

Samuel Smith's Taddy Porter. A beer which is notable for being brewed in Yorkshire, a pale ale town, and for being widely available (and remarkably expensive) in the United States. It is nicely carbonated, not too gassy, and forms a firm long-lasting head. It is slightly translucent with a pleasing red hue and is reasonably well-balanced, very dry, but with perhaps just a little too much black malt roastiness. This is still a pretty good porter, even though it costs much more here than it should!

7

Further Reading

Since porter is a beer so rich in history, some of you may be interested in reading more about it. I am only going to give you a limited number of references; there is just not enough space to list *all* my sources, many of which are scattered through a multitude of magazine articles and books. In addition, many of the books I have used are either out of print or very difficult to find.

If you are interested, Michael Jackson's book, and that of H. S. Corran, are the best places to start, and the others in this short list should give you plenty to be getting on with:

Baron, Stanley, *Brewed in America*, 1962, Little, Brown and Company Inc., New York.

Campaign For Real Ale, *Good Beer Guide 1991*, 1991, St. Albans, Herts., England.

Clark, Peter, *The English Alehouse*, 1983, Longman, Inc., New York.

Corran, H. S., *A History of Brewing*, 1975, David & Charles Inc., North Pomfret, Vermont.

Eckhardt, Fred, *The Essentials of Beer Style*, 1989, All Brewers Information Service, Portland, Oregon.

Girouard, Mark, *Victorian Pubs*, 1984, Yale University Press, New Haven, Connecticut.

Hawkins, K. H., and C. L. Pass, *The Brewing Industry*, 1979, Heinemann, London.

Jackson, Michael, *The New World Guide to Beer*, 1988, Running Press Book Publishers, Philadelphia, Pennsylvania.

Kenna, Rudolph, and Anthony Mooney, *People's Palaces*, 1983, Paul Harris Publishing, Edinburgh, Scotland.

King, F. A., *Beer Has A History*, 1947, Hutchinson's, London.

Monckton, H. A., *A History of English Ale and Beer*, 1966, The Bodley Head, London.

Monckton, H. A., *A History of The English Public House*, 1969, The Bodley Head, London.

Protz, Roger, *The Real Ale Drinker's Almanac*, 1989, Lochar Publishing, Moffat, Scotland.

Spiller, Brian, *Victorian Public Houses*, 1972, David & Charles, Newton Abbot, Devon, England.

Vaizey, John, *The Brewing Industry 1886-1951*, 1960, Sir Isaac Pitman & Sons, London.

Glossary

adjunct. Any *unmalted* grain or other fermentable ingredient added to the mash.

aeration. The action of introducing air to the wort at various stages of the brewing process.

airlock. (see fermentation lock)

airspace. (see ullage)

alcohol by volume (v/v). The percentage of volume of alcohol per volume of beer. To calculate the approximate volumetric alcohol content, subtract the terminal gravity from the original gravity and divide the result by 75. For example: 1.050 - 1.012 = .038 / 75 = 5% v/v.

alcohol by weight (w/v). The percentage weight of alcohol per volume of beer. For example: 3.2% alcohol by weight = 3.2 grams of alcohol per 100 centiliters of beer.

ale. 1. Historically, an unhopped malt beverage. 2. Now a generic term for hopped beers produced by top fermentation, as opposed to lagers, which are produced by bottom fermentation.

all-extract beer. A beer made with only malt extract as opposed to one made from barley, or a combination of malt extract and barley.

all-grain beer. A beer made with only malted barley as opposed to one made from malt extract, or from malt extract and malted barley.

all-malt beer. A beer made with only barley malt with no adjuncts or refined sugars.

alpha acid. A soft resin in hop cones. When boiled, alpha acids are converted to iso-alpha-acids, which account for 60 percent of a beer's bitterness.

alpha-acid unit. A measurement of the potential bitterness of hops, expressed by their percentage of alpha acid. Low = 2 to 4%, medium = 5 to 7%, high = 8 to 12%. Abbrev: A.A.U.

attenuation. The reduction in the wort's specific gravity caused by the transformation of sugars into alcohol and carbon-dioxide gas.

Balling. A saccharometer invented by Carl Joseph Napoleon Balling in 1843. It is calibrated for 63.5 degrees F (17.5 degrees C), and graduated in grams per hundred, giving a direct reading of the percentage of extract by weight per 100 grams solution. For example: 10 °B = 10 grams of sugar per 100 grams of wort.

blow-by (blow-off). A single-stage homebrewing fermentation method in which a plastic tube is fitted into the mouth of a carboy, with the other end submerged in a pail of sterile water. Unwanted residues and carbon dioxide are expelled through the tube, while air is prevented from coming into contact with the fermenting beer, thus avoiding contamination.

carbonation. The process of introducing carbon-dioxide gas into a liquid by: 1. injecting the finished beer with carbon dioxide; 2. adding young fermenting beer to finished beer for a renewed fermentation (kraeusening); 3. priming (adding sugar) to fermented wort prior to bottling, creating a secondary fermentation in the bottle.

carboy. A large glass, plastic or earthenware bottle.

chill haze. Haziness caused by protein and tannin during the secondary fermentation.

dry hopping. The addition of hops to the primary fermenter, the secondary fermenter, or to casked beer to add aroma and hop character to the finished beer without adding significant bitterness.

dry malt. Malt extract in powdered form.

extract. The amount of dissolved materials in the wort after mashing and lautering malted barley and/or malt adjuncts such as corn and rice.

fermentation lock. A one-way valve, which allows carbon-dioxide gas to escape from the fermenter while excluding contaminants.

final specific gravity. The specific gravity of a beer when fermentation is complete.

fining. The process of adding clarifying agents to beer during secondary fermentation to precipitate suspended matter.

flocculation. The behavior of yeast cells joining into masses and settling out toward the end of fermentation.

homebrew bittering units. A formula invented by the American Homebrewers Association to measure bitterness of beer. Example: 1.5 ounces of hops at 10 percent alpha acid for five gallons: 1.5 x 10 = 15 HBU per five gallons.

hop pellets. Finely powdered hop cones compressed into tablets. Hop pellets are 20 to 30 percent more bitter by weight than the same variety in loose form.

hydrometer. A glass instrument used to measure the specific gravity of liquids as compared to water, consisting of a graduated stem resting on a weighed float.

International bitterness units. This is an empirical quantity which was originally designed to measure the concentration of iso-alpha-acids in milligrams per liter (parts per million). Most procedures will also measure a small amount of uncharacterized soft resins so IBUs are generally 5 to 100% higher than iso-alpha acid concentrations.

isinglass. A gelatinous substance made from the swim bladder of certain fish and added to beer as a fining agent.

kraeusen. (n.) The rocky head of foam which appears on the surface of the wort during fermentation. (v.) To add fermenting wort to fermented beer to induce carbonation through a secondary fermentation.

lager. (n.) A generic term for any bottom-fermented beer. Lager brewing is now the predominant brewing method worldwide except in Britain where top fermented ales dominate. (v.) To store beer at near-zero temperatures in order to precipitate yeast cells and proteins and improve taste.

lauter tun. A vessel in which the mash settles and the grains are removed from the sweet wort through a straining process. It has a false, slotted bottom and spigot.

liquefaction. The process by which alpha-amylase enzymes degrade soluble starch into dextrin.

malt. Barley that has been steeped in water, germinated, then dried in kilns. This process converts insoluble starchs to soluble substances and sugars.

malt extract. A thick syrup or dry powder prepared from malt.

mashing. Mixing ground malt with water to extract the fermentables, degrade haze-forming proteins and convert grain starches to fermentable sugars and nonfermentable carbohydrates.

modification. 1. The physical and chemical changes in barley as a result of malting. 2. The degree to which these changes have occured, as determined by the growth of the acrospire.

original gravity. The specific gravity of wort previous to fermentation. A measure of the total amount of dissolved solids in wort.

pH. A measure of acidity or alkalinity of a solution, usually on a scale of one to 14, where seven is neutral.

Plato. A saccharometer that expresses specific gravity as extract weight in a one-hundred-gram solution at 68 degrees F (20 degrees C). A revised, more accurate version of Balling, developed by Dr. Plato.

primary fermentation. The first stage of fermentation, during which most fermentable sugars are converted to ethyl alcohol and carbon dioxide.

priming sugar. A small amount of corn, malt or cane sugar added to bulk beer prior to racking or at bottling to induce a new fermentation and create carbonation.

racking. The process of transferring beer from one container to another, especially into the final package (bottles, kegs, etc.).

saccharification. The naturally occurring process in which malt starch is converted into fermentable sugars, primarily maltose.

saccharometer. An instrument that determines the sugar concentration of a solution by measuring the specific gravity.

secondary fermentation. 1. The second, slower stage of fermentation, lasting from a few weeks to many months depending on the type of beer. 2. A fermentation occuring in bottles or casks and initiated by priming or by adding yeast.

sparging. Spraying the spent grains in the mash with hot water to retrieve the remaining malt sugar.

specific gravity. A measure of a substance's density as compared to that of water, which is given the value of 1.000 at 39.2 degrees F (4 degrees C). Specific gravity has no accompanying units, because it is expressed as a ratio.

starter. A batch of fermenting yeast, added to the wort to initiate fermentation.

strike temperature. The initial temperature of the water when the malted barley is added to it to create the mash.

trub. Suspended particles resulting from the precipitation of proteins, hop oils and tannins during boiling and cooling stages of brewing.

ullage. The empty space between a liquid and the top of its container. Also called airspace or headspace.

v/v: (see alcohol by volume)

w/v: (see alcohol by weight)

water hardness. The degree of dissolved minerals in water.

wort. The mixture that results from mashing the malt and boiling the hops, before it is fermented into beer.

Index

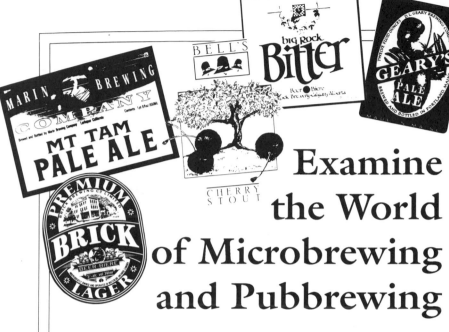

Examine the World of Microbrewing and Pubbrewing

Travel the world of commercial, small-scale brewing; the realm of microbrewers and pubbrewers.

The New Brewer magazine guides you through this new industry. Its pages introduce you to marketing, finance, operations, equipment, recipes, interviews—in short, the whole landscape.

Subscribe to *The New Brewer* and become a seasoned traveler.

NO RISK OFFER

Subscribe now and receive six issues.
If you're not completely satisfied, we'll refund you completely.

$55 a year (U.S.) $65 (Foreign)

Published by The Institute for Brewing Studies, PO Box 1510, Boulder, CO 80306-1510, (303) 447-0816

The New Brewer

THE MAGAZINE FOR MICRO AND PUB-BREWERS

Books for your Brewing Library. . .
from Brewers Publications

All prices are quoted in U.S. dollars. Prices may change and shipping charges vary. For information, write or call: Association of Brewers, PO Box 1679, Boulder, CO 80306-1679 USA. Telephone (303) 447-0816, FAX (303) 447-2825.

Dictionary of Beer and Brewing

This valuable reference will make an outstanding contribution to any brewing library! Author Carl Forget has compiled 1,929 essential definitions used in beermaking, including: Brewing Processes • Ingredients • Types and Styles of Beer • Abbreviations • Arcane Terms • Also: Conversion Tables for temperatures, alcohol percentages and factors.

6 x 0, 180 pp.   **Suggested retail price $19.95**

Brewing Lager Beer

This classic reference book is a must for serious brewers interested in all-grain brewing and recipes. First, author Greg Noonan describes the brewing process and ingredients in plain English. Then he guides you through planning and brewing seven classic lager beers — including recipes. As a bonus, the tables of brewing information are excellent.

5 1/2 x 8 1/2, 320 pp. 4th Printing.   **Suggested retail price $14.95**

Brewing Mead

Mead is a wonderful honey wine with great, untapped commercial value. Charlie Papazian gives step-by-step recipes and instructions for making several varieties of this honey-based brew. Mead was the beverage of royalty in Europe and was reportedly a powerful aphrodisiac. Lt. Col. Robert Gayre of Scotland gives its history. Now is the time to discover the exotic secrets of mead.

5 1/2 x 8 1/2, 200 pp. 2nd Printing.   **Suggested retail price $11.95**

Best of Beer and Brewing

From the transcripts of the 1982-1985 Conferences on Beer and Brewing

Rather than reprint all four transcripts, we chose the very best 15 talks from the four Conferences, asked the authors to update them, and compiled them in one valuable, affordable volume.

5 1/2 x 8 1/2, 260 pp.   **Suggested retail price $17.95**

Beer and Brewing, Vol. 7

Transcript of the 1987 Conference on Quality Beer and Brewing

This collection gives readers the widest range of beer information ever published in a single volume. Suited for commercial and homebrewers. Its 17 chapters include: Yeast Strain Traits • Recipe Formulation • Brewing to Scale • Brewing in Your Environs • Origin of Beer Flavor • Innovations in Equipment • Beer Folklore • Contemporary Brewing • Plus ten more.

5 1/2 x 8 1/2, 237 pp.   **Suggested retail price $20.95**

Beer and Brewing, Vol. 8
Transcript of the 1988 Conference on Quality Beer and Brewing

There's a world of beer in this transcript, from practical brewing techniques to a perspective of beers abroad given by European brewers. Chapters include: Improved Record-Keeping • Practical All-Grain Brewing • Aroma ID Kit Development • Making Amazing Mead • Brewpubs in Austria.

5 1/2 x 8 1/2, 220 pp. **Suggested retail price $20.95**

Beer and Brewing, Vol. 9
Transcript of the 1989 Conference on Quality Beer and Brewing

Here are the transcripts from the biggest AHA Conference ever. This exciting book recaptures the spirit of the event and overflows with invaluable tips in each of its 13 chapters, including: What Makes an Ale an Ale • Clear Beer Please! • Hop Madness • Applying Science to the Art of Brewing.

5 1/2 x 8 1/2, 247 pp. **Suggested retail price $20.95**

Beer and Brewing, Vol. 10
Transcript of the 1990 Conference on Quality Beer and Brewing

Read all the talks that made four days in Oakland the ultimate homebrew experience. A dozen talks all focused on the quality of beer and beermaking. Chapters include: Beer Blending ala Judy • Slings of Outrageous Fortune • The World of Malt • Carbonating Your Brew • Home Laboratory Culturing.

5 1/2 x 8 1/2, 198 pp. **Suggested retail price $20.95**

Brew Free or Die! Beer and Brewing, Vol. 11
Transcript of the 1991 Conference on Quality Beer and Brewing

Brew Free or Die! Beer and Brewing, Vol. 11 gives the homebrewer a wealth of knowledge about brewing, from techniques to recipes, gadgets, computerization and much more. Find out what the experts shared at the 1991 AHA Homebrew Conference in this readable collection of papers. Terry Foster explores pale ale, Greg Noonan counsels on brewing water, Candy Schermerhorn shares her secrets for cooking with beer, and an additional host of experts give their hard-won knowledge in this informative book.

5 1/2 x 8 1/2, 239 pp. **Suggested retail price $20.95**

Brewery Operations, Vol. 3
1986 Microbrewers Conference Transcript

The Brewery Operations series books provide practical, tried-and-true suggestions for small-scale brewing and marketing. Chapters include: Wort Production • Marketing the Pubbrewery • Contract Brewing • Yeast and Fermentation • Brewery Public Relations • Cottage Brewing.

5 1/2 x 8 1/2, 180 pp. **Suggested retail price $25.95**

Brewery Operations, Vol. 4
1987 Microbrewers Conference Transcript

Expert information on brewing, marketing, engineering and management. Chapters include: Malt Extract in Microbrewing • Techniques of Major Breweries • Engineering for the Microbrewer • Developing a Marketing Plan • How to Hire Good People • Equipment Systems for the Brewpub • BATF Regulations.
5 1/2 x 8 1/2, 210 pp.   **Suggested retail price $25.95**

Brewery Operations, Vol. 5
1988 Microbrewers Conference Transcript

Are you a brewpub operator, just getting into the industry or thinking of expanding? Then you'll want to know every fact in *Brewery Operations, Vol. 5.* There were 21 specialized presentations (27 speakers in all) at the 1988 Conference, providing practical information for all brewers. Topics include: Brewery Feasibility Studies • Equipment Design Considerations • Franchising • Working with Distributors • Yeast Handling • Product Development • Expanding Your Brewery.
5 1/2 x 8 1/2, 330 pp.   **Suggested retail price $25.95**

Brewery Operations, Vol. 6
1989 Microbrewers Conference Transcript

Your guide to the rapidly changing environment of pub- and microbreweries. Chapters include: Legislative Initiatives • Handling Regulatory Authorities • Beer Packaging Design • Working with Distributors • Quality Assurance Systems • Current Federal Regulations • Offering Other's Beers.
5 1/2 x 8 1/2, 205 pp.   **Suggested retail price $25.95**

Brewery Operations, Vol. 7
1990 Microbrewers Conference Transcript

Brewery Operations, Vol. 7, the transcripts of the Denver Conference for microbrewers and pubbrewers, reviews the world of the new commercial brewer. Subjects in the published transcripts include Jeff Mendel's industry overview; Charlie Papazian's presentation on off-flavors; Fred Scheer, of Frankenmuth Brewery, on bottling; Dan Gordon, of Gordon Biersch Brewpub, on trub; Al Geitner, of Pub Brewing Co., on alternative beverages for the brewpub; John Foley, of Connecticut Brewing Co., on strategic plan for contract brewers and Dan Carey, of J.V. Northwest, on microbrewery design performance.
5 1/2 x 8 1/2, 212 pp.   **Suggested retail price $25.95**

Brewing Under Adversity
Brewery Operations, Vol. 8
1991 Microbrewers Conference Transcripts

It is more difficult than ever to run a successful brewing business in today's climate of anti-alcohol sentiment and restrictive legislation. The 1991 Microbrewers Conference, titled "Brewing Under Adversity," addressed this topic and many others pertaining to the smaller brewing venture, and *Brewing Under Adversity, Brewery Operations, Vol, 8* brings this information to you. Topics include: Brewing Under Adversity, Industry Overview, Packaging for the Environment, Brewpub Design Efficiency and Operating Multiple Units.
5 1/2 x 8 1/2, 246 pp.   Suggested retail price $25.95

Brewers Resource Directory

Here are the updated phone numbers, addresses, personnel and descriptions of North American breweries and suppliers you've been waiting for! We know how valuable this publication is by the thousands sold to date. It's the most definitive directory in the industry. You get complete listings for: Microbreweries and Brewpubs • Ingredient Suppliers • Brewing Consultants • Equipment Manufacturers • Large Breweries • Associations and Publications • State Laws and Excise Taxes. Updated and published yearly. Includes a revised and expanded beer styles chapter.

Plus, an informative article and statistics summarizing the year's activities and trends.
8 1/2 x 11, 281 pp.   Suggested retail price $80.00

Brewery Planner
A Guide to Opening Your Own Small Brewery

When planning to open a brewery, it only makes sense to find out everything you can from those who have already learned about the business, sometimes the hard way. *Brewery Planner* is designed to prepare the new brewer for every potential obstacle or necessity. It is a collection of articles written by experienced brewers, covering The Physical Plant in Section One, Tips from the Experts in Section Two, Marketing and Distribution in Section Three, and Business Plan, Including Templates for Financial Statements in Section Four. A must for anyone planning to open a brewery.
8 1/2 x 11, 191 pp.   Suggested retail price $70.00

The Winners Circle

There is no other book like it! 126 award-winning homebrew recipes for 21 styles of lager, ale, and mead.

Start brewing with this refreshing collection of tried-and-true homebrew recipes selected from the winners of the AHA National Homebrew Competition.
5 1/2 x 8 1/2, 298 pp.   Suggested retail price $11.95

Principles of Brewing Science

George Fix has created a masterful look at the chemistry and biochemistry of brewing. With a helpful short course in the appendix, this book will unravel the mysteries of brewing, showing you what really goes on during the making of beer and how you can improve it. An absolute must for those who want to get the most out of their brewing.

5 1/2 x 8 1/2, 250 pp.   Suggested retail price $29.95

Pale Ale

First in the Classic Beer Style Series

Terry Foster, a British expatriate and renowned expert on British beers has created a technical masterpiece on pale ale, the world's most popular style of ale. Written with an entertaining historical perspective, this book more than measures up to its subject matter.

Chapters include history, character, flavor, ingredients, brewing, methods and comparisons of commercial pale ales.

5 1/2 x 8 1/2, 140 pp.   Suggested retail price $11.95

Continental Pilsener

Second in the Classic Beer Style Series

Learn the ingredients and techniques that produce this golden, distinctively hopped lager. Dave Miller, an award-winning brewer and author, takes you through the history, flavor, ingredients and methods of the beer that revolutionized brewing.

You'll also learn about current commercial examples of the style. Professionals and homebrewers alike will enjoy this exploration of a classic beer.

5 1/2 x 8 1/2, 102 pp.   Suggested retail price $11.95

Lambic

Third in the Classic Beer Style Series

Lambic, by Jean-Xavier Guinard, is the only book ever published that completely examines this exotic and elusive style. From origins to brewing techniques, *Lambic* unravels the mysteries that make this rare style so popular. *Lambic* contains the only directory of the lambic breweries of Belgium. Guinard, a student of Dr. Michael Lewis at the University of California at Davis, grew up in the shadow of lambic breweries and combined vocation and avocation to produce this wonderful book.

5 1/2 x 8 1/2, 169 pp.   Suggested retail price $11.95

Vienna, Märzen, Oktoberfest
Fourth in the Classic Beer Style Series

Vienna, a dark, delicious lager, has never been easier to brew. George Fix, well known homebrewer and beer scientist, and his wife, Laurie, explore the history and techniques of this style, giving recipes and in-depth instructions.

Brewers have long known that this is a difficult beer to make true to style—but *Vienna*, the first book to explore this lager, helps even beginning brewers master it.

5 1/2 x 8/12, approx. 160 pp.   **Suggested retail price $11.95**

Belgian Ale
Sixth in the Classic Beer Style Series

Discover the amazing complexity of Belgian ale with Pierre Rajotte. His passion for unique, flavorful beers has led him on a lifetime journey and taken him around the world in search of the ultimate brew. Follow along as Rajotte takes you on a journey of discovery in Belgium. Learn how Belgium's ethnic diversity has spawned more than 600 brands of beer. Rajotte teaches the importance of sugar, Belgian hops and top fermenting yeasts in the Belgian ale tradition. After reading *Belgian Ale* you'll be ready to brew your own Belgian-style, high gravity beer.

5 1/2 x 8 1/2, approx. 175 pp.   **Suggested retail price $11.95**

PORTER

Porter takes readers into the history of the beer
George Washington brewed with step-by-step
instructions to create this rich, full-bodied beer.
Porter by Terry Foster is the only in-depth book to
guide readers in brewing this style with modern
ingredients and equipment.

Terry Foster is the author of *Pale Ale* (Brewers
Publications). He has been brewing for over 30
years in both England and the United States.

*"Elusive, shadowy, dark...porter excercises a fascination
over all beer lovers. Tenacious Terry Foster has tracked this
mysterious brew almost obsessively."*

MICHAEL JACKSON
author of *The World Guide to Beer*
and *Pocket Guide to Beer*

*"There are advantages to having Terry Foster write this
book. First, he's British, but lived in America for some
time—an advantage for someone trying to elucidate an
essentially British topic for American readers. Second, Terry
has long been interested in the evolution of the porter style,
not ultimately as an historian, but as a brewer."*

BYRON BURCH
Brewing Quality Beer

The Classic Beer Style Series from Brewers
Publications examines individual world-class beer
styles, covering origins, history, sensory profiles,
brewing techniques and commercial examples.

A Brewers Publications Book

ISBN 0-937381-28-4

9 780937 381281